Snow & The Ladies of Petros United Methodist Church

❄

by
June Patrick Gibbs

TENNESSEE VALLEY
Publishing
Knoxville, Tennessee
2004

Copyright © 2004

All rights reserved. No part of this book may be reproduced in any form or by any electronic or mechanical means including information storage and retrieval systems without permission in writing from the author, except by a reviewer, who may quote brief passages in a review.

Published by:
    Tennessee Valley Publishing
    PO Box 52527
    Knoxville, Tennessee 37950-2527

Printed and bound in the United States of America.

Library of Congress Control Number: 2004112196

ISBN: 193260412X

Scripture taken from the HOLY BIBLE, NEW INTERNATIONAL VERSION®. Copyright © 1973, 1978, 1984 by International Bible Society. Used by permission of Zondervan Publishing House. All rights reserved.

Photo Credits: The author is grateful to the Roane County Heritage Commission for permission to use pictures of Petros, ca. 1908, from the T.C. Farnham Collection, and to the *Morgan County News* for providing pictures published in news articles about Polly Woodward. All other photos are provided courtesy of the subjects of this book or are from the author's collection.

---

*This book is dedicated to
Casey (6/3/82 - 7/25/96)
who loved "Granny's church."*

To Mom, Polly, Miss Imogene and Miss Whitus: The way you live your faith gives the rest of us strength. Thank you for allowing me to spend time with you and for reminding me that I'm glad you were and are a part of my life.

To Nikki and Erin and the beautiful grandchildren you have given me: Thank you for just being. You make me glad to be alive.

And,

To Steve: Thank you for loving me, for watering and feeding me, and for making it possible for me to write and publish this book.

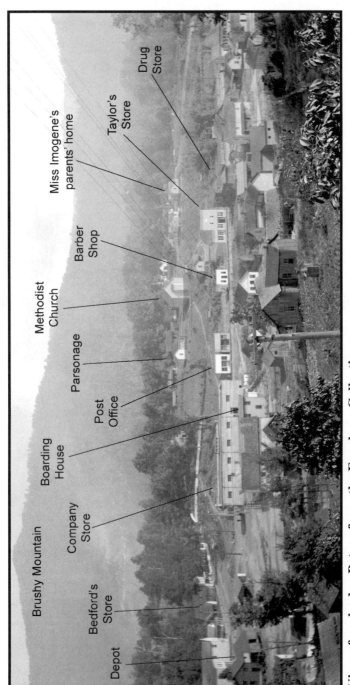

View of early-day Petros from the Farnham Collection.

CONTENTS

Introduction vii

Polly Rogers Whaley Woodward 1

Imogene Nelle Whitus Evans 45

Alice Lucille Bullock Whitus 75

Lucy Alice Duncan Patrick 113

Photograph Gallery 151

The Town 175

The Church 177

The Penitentiary 183

Bibliography 189

In fall, we learn how old age can be beautiful, and that letting go doesn't mean giving up. In winter, we see patience at work, and if we try, we can hear secrets the woods tell only in winter, and only to those who listen.

– Ina Hughs

INTRODUCTION

My mother's 80th birthday was approaching in July 1999 when I walked into the Petros United Methodist Church to prepare for a surprise birthday party my family would host there in her honor later in the month. No one was in the church that afternoon, and I could just take my time wandering around and losing myself in memories. It had been a few years since I had been inside this church, but it was so easy to remember who sat where . . . the verses to songs we used to sing . . . the little prayer we always said as we were dismissed.

It was easy to remember my mother following along in her Sunday School book as the teacher spoke. It took no effort to recall Polly ringing the bell at the top of the steps to let the children in the classes downstairs know it was time to come upstairs, or to recall her changing the ATTENDANCE and COLLECTION numbers on the board at the front of the church. The melodies of songs Miss Imogene played on the piano each Sunday still seemed to echo inside the church, and I could still hear them in my mind. As I looked at the lectern where Miss Whitus always stood when she taught the Sunday School class, I could remember the dresses she wore and how she sometimes closed her eyes when she spoke. The love inside that church was palpable.

The warm feeling that visit evoked stayed with me. The more I thought about my mom, Polly, Miss Imogene and Miss Whitus, the more I realized what really special women they are. They have led quiet but interesting, eventful lives in a rural area. They are all dedicated to their church, their town and to each other. They are in their 80s and 90s now, but they are very much alive and engaged in the world.

What you are about to read are stories from their lives, told in their words, with their voices. I have made my best effort to be true to what they told me in interviews and to reflect what I saw in their eyes and heard in their voices as they recalled their 85-plus years of life.

I call these ladies the "Snow Blossoms." That name came about on one cold February day as Polly and I were driving to my mother's house. I mentioned that the tops of the mountains around Petros were beautiful that day. You couldn't tell where the tree tops ended and the sky began. The snow-clad mountain peaks that surrounded us were literally sparkling as the sun shone on the ice crystals. Polly said, "Oh, those are snow blossoms. That's what the old-timers call the frozen snow on the trees back up on the high points. They look like flowers. On Friday, from here to Wartburg, they came down to the highway. The whole mountains were that way. They were beautiful. Oh, gee, it was just like heaven. You'd just think you were in another world."

I thought of the similarities between these ladies and snow blossoms, and I knew immediately that Polly had just named this book. These ladies, like snow blossoms, are at the top of the mountain. They're beautiful. They sparkle. And there were times in their lives when they blossomed in spite of snow.

The four "Snow Blossoms" have known each other for a long time, through good times and bad. The ties that bind them are strong. I have included information about some of these ties – their church, their town and even the prison in their town – in the back of this book. I thought about putting that information in the front, but I decided against it because it is the "Snow Blossoms" themselves who are the real story.

Snow Blossoms

The Ladies
of
Petros United
Methodist Church

POLLY ROGERS WHALEY WOODWARD

FAMILY

My name is – do I have to say it? It is Laura Pauline Rogers. That was my two grandmothers' names. Laura was my daddy's mother, and Pauline was my Grandma Bardill's name. And I had a little old aunt named Pauline. She didn't like me, and I didn't like her. That's why I don't like the name Pauline. I never did like my name. Nobody ever calls me Pauline. It sounds funny. My sister Velma and my mother started calling me "Polly" when I was just real young.

Polly.

My mother's name was Emma Margaret Bardill. My Grandmother Bardill was a Goldberg. The Goldbergs came from Germany, and the Bardills came from Switzerland. They lived in Mossy Grove, Tennessee. Where the stores are, the markets and everything, you turn in there on the old Mossy Grove Road and turn to the right. Right there, where that road is, was the beginning of their farm. It went all the way down to what they called "Dug Hollow." That first curve when you go around that – their farm went to right there. My Uncle Ed – the Goldbergs – lived on the other side of the road. I don't know if that was all the same farm, whether it belonged to the Bardills or the Goldbergs. I'd like to find out.

My mother's sister lived almost at the end of that farm. She had six boys. They moved to Indiana. I remember that old barn. I looked the other day. That old barn is still standing. And that house they built is still there; it doesn't look bad. But they tore my grandmother's house down. It was a log house, but they put the boards on the outside and you wouldn't know it was log. I'd love to know who bought the logs. I'd love to have had them and built me a little log house right there *[next to her house in Petros]*. I can still remember that big old two-story house. It had great big old walnut trees in the yard. And that one across the road where my uncle lived had two big walnut trees in each corner of the yard. That tornado in November 2002 blew them over. Oh, it just broke my

Baby Polly with older sister Velma and older brother John.

heart cause my grandmother had that big one in her yard and we used to have picnics under there. Every summer the Rogers family had a picnic under that walnut tree at my grandmother's or down at Aunt Minnie Heidel's house. Every summer we had that picnic. We'd go to Laymance Falls or Potter's Falls. The Heidels – there was a whole bunch of them. This one family of Heidels used to come up here all the time. Katie was my good friend, and Clarence. Two of the boys of that family are still living, Martin and Edwin. We're "hugging friends."

We've done a lot of genealogy on the Bardills, but I can't do much with the Goldbergs. My Great-Grandfather Goldberg was buried in that old Lutheran cemetery up on the hill in Wartburg. Then when they built that bypass, they took those bones up and put them in one great grave down in the main cemetery. They didn't put any names on it, so you don't know who's who. But my great-grandfather was in that bunch. My great-grandmother was buried at Liberty beside her deaf and dumb son. I've seen that grave. They had stones, but evidently they fell over and they've just hauled them off. I can't find the grave now. If I could, I would put up a marker.

My father's full name was William Peter Rogers. My father was born in Marietta, Georgia, but he was raised in Murphy, North Carolina. He was going through the country with some surveyors, and they were down at Mossy Grove. They were boarding with a Langley family. My mother and the Langleys' daughter Emma – both of them were named Emma – Emma Langley and Emma Bardill – ran around together. The surveyors, when they didn't have anything to do, wanted to go over to visit them one night. They said, "Well, they've got two good-looking girls." They went. My mother played the guitar and sang. My dad's name was Bill. Of course she didn't know what his name was, and she sang a funny song: "He urges me to wed him, but I hardly think I will" – and it went all through and at the last it said, "So I think I'll marry Bill." They kidded her about it. When she found out his name was Bill, it was so embarrassing to her.

Bill Rogers stayed in the area because Emma Bardill was there.

He went to work up at the prison in Petros. He ran around with Bill Boone. Bill Boone was his buddy. Bill was going with a young girl down around Union, and my daddy, of course, was dating my mama. So Bill told him, said, "You go with me one Sunday. I'll get you a date with this other girl." And he did. Then the next Sunday, they came down to Mossy Grove and Dad went with my mama, and Bill Boone went with her friend Emma. And my mama found out about the other girl. So she said, "You can either go with that old girl or me. You make up your mind which one you want." He wanted my mama, so they got married.

Local people refer to Brushy Mountain Penitentiary in Petros, and the property surrounding it where state employees live, as "the state." The town of Petros and "the state" in some ways used to be like two separate communities.

When my mother married and moved here, and Daddy was working up there at the prison, there was a row of houses up there by the reservoir at the prison, across from the warden's house. They called it "Stith Row." They lived on "Stith Row." I don't know where the name Stith Row came from. All the houses at the state were painted red. All the state – everything – was painted barn red. The old prison was painted barn red. That other row of houses was called "Georgia Row" because all those people came here from Georgia to work at the prison – like the Bedfords, the Metcalfs, the Patricks, the Beenes. All those people. They called it "Georgia Row."

Then they bought the house across the road from where I live now, and we lived there the rest of the time. When I wasn't out gadding about, I was there.

Bill and Emma Rogers had two daughters and four sons. Polly will only say that April 16 is her birthday; she won't say what year she was born.

Velma was the oldest, and then John, then me, then Elbert, Glenn and Hugh.

John drowned in Lake Santeetlah, North Carolina, when he was a young man.

John worked for the Tennessee Valley Authority (TVA). He was an electrician. He fixed the switch that President Roosevelt used to turn on the lights at Norris Dam. He was helping build the Fontana Dam. He worked on the Fontana and the Hiwassee, both dams. He and two other men went fishing – Lake Santeetlah – and the boat turned over. He was a good swimmer, but he had on heavy clothes. It was cold. The other two, one of them could hardly swim, but he got out. But they said John went down. They held onto the boat for awhile, and then they decided to swim for it. Of course that water is so cold up there in the mountain. And those heavy clothes – I think he had boots on. But they said one of them said, "John, are you going to make it?" and he shook his head. Said he never did speak. We always thought he had a heart attack, because he had a bad heart.

I don't know how old John was when he died. My brother Elbert was in the service in Marianna, Florida, and I was staying down there with his family. We got the message the day they brought Jeanne, my niece, home from the hospital when she was born. We didn't have time to get gas. It was rationed. We could have driven, but we didn't have time to go through all that to get the gas. So we tried to get a plane, and we could get to Atlanta but we couldn't get from Atlanta to Knoxville. So we had to take the bus. It was so crowded with soldiers and everything. Elbert's wife took us to the bus station, and she told the bus driver what had happened. Whenever they got off for a rest stop, when he got ready to put them back on the bus, he let us get on first. Of course the ones that had come in on the bus would get their seat back, you know, but the rest of the ones just getting on there didn't. But he let us get on because he knew that I couldn't stand up. I was so sick. I lay with my head in Elbert's lap nearly all the way home. My head was splitting. And I'm not going to tell you what happened. I don't believe I want that on the record. We got to Columbus, Georgia, and changed buses. I was so sick, and I hadn't eaten all day either. He took his little ditty bag that he had on the bus, and he went across the street to a liquor store and got some apricot brandy. He brought it back, and he said, "Take this to the restroom, and you take a big swallow of this. I'm not going to get you home if you don't." And I did, but it didn't help. But we got home in enough time for the funeral.

My brother Glenn was the dentist who lived in Knoxville. He had a heart condition from a child. He had rheumatic heart. We kept after Glenn all the time. But it was hard. He said he'd rather have a short life and do some things he wanted to do than have a long life and not be able to do anything. He went to college. He played football, and they put him in the hospital. His daughter D.G., when she came home, she said, "Daddy's been in the hospital." We said, "Why? What was wrong with him?" "He was playing football." He couldn't swim because we wouldn't let him go in swimming. He'd get purple. I was down there in Florida when Glenn died too. I said they were going to quit letting me go to Florida cause every time I went . . .

Polly's sister Velma retired as a school teacher from the Oak Ridge City School System and moved to Tucson, Arizona. She died in 1990. Polly's youngest brother Hugh retired as a teacher/principal in West Tennessee. He died of prostate cancer in 1995.

Kids loved Hugh to death. He started using a newspaper. A lot of them made a big to-do over teaching out of the newspaper, but now they really do believe in it. He's the first I'd ever heard do it.

Hugh and Ridley Kennedy grew up together here. They climbed trees. Hugh had a tree house, and he'd pull Ridley up. He'd tie a rope around his waist and pull him up in the tree. Hugh was always a kid. You didn't know what he was going to do. I miss him more than any because he was always there for me. When I had my hysterectomy, he stayed day and night for several days. When I broke my hip, it was about three o'clock in the afternoon, and the doctor said, "I can do it tonight, or I can wait until in the morning." I said, "Do it tonight so I won't have to worry about it all night." Of course, I was kind of in shock anyway and didn't know what I was saying. The next morning – I didn't wake up until the next morning – there's old Hugh standing by my bed. I said, "Where did you come from?" He said, "I was here for your surgery." He lived in Georgia. There he was.

Now there's just Elbert and me left. Elbert retired from TVA as an instrument mechanic. He took our sister Velma to Farmington, New Mexico, and then to Tucson, Arizona, for her health after she retired. He stayed in Arizona and worked for Arizona Power and Light Company. Then he retired again and came back to live in Jasper, Tennessee. He lives in Athens, Tennessee, now.

CHILDHOOD MEMORIES

You know, it seemed a long way then from Petros to Mossy Grove. We used to go out there to my grandma's about every Sunday. But that seemed like such a far way. I went to church down there when I'd be at my grandma's. They had church in the old schoolhouse at first, and then they built a church. We all walked because nobody had many cars.

My daddy had an old Maxwell car, his first car. You never saw a Maxwell, because that was the only one I saw. Bruno Schubert – the Schuberts out at Wartburg – had the agency for it, this old car. It had side curtains. It didn't have roll-down windows. My daddy chewed tobacco. He chewed that tobacco, and he would spit the ambeer out. Whoever was sitting on that side, in the back, got the ambeer. I dreaded it.

Daddy never could drive. He scared us to death. He hated driving. And none of us was old enough to drive. He was tickled to death when John got old enough to drive and he didn't have to. Later, when I could drive, no matter how fast I went, he never said to slow down. But my mama, if you got 30 miles an hour – "Polly, your foot's getting too heavy." She watched the speedometer. But Dad would never say, "Slow down." He never told me to slow down. But she sure did.

Glenn had a project in school out at Wartburg. He planted tomatoes. Mr. Lesley had a little farm down Cassell Road. I'd never been down there, but Glenn wanted my mama and me to go down to see his tomato patch. So I drove. Glenn couldn't drive yet. I was going pretty fast on this little old country road – just two ruts, it wasn't a road – and all at once I looked straight down. It looked like it was forever to the foot of that hill, a steep hill, and my mother said, "Oh, Polly, throw it in something!" We had the gears down here, and she wanted me to slow it down, put it in low, you know, and slow it down. She couldn't think what it was, so she said, "Oh, Polly, throw it in something!" And I threw it in something and slowed down.

Polly said she learned to drive, sitting under an oak tree at her house. Her mother ("Emmy") insisted that one of her brothers accompany her on her first test drive.

I learned low, high, reverse. I sat out there and I learned to do the gears. So I said, "Emmy, I'm going to take the car off the hill." And she said, "Well, don't do it by yourself. Let one of the boys go with you." I said, "I don't want one of the boys to go with me." John was there that day – he lived in North Carolina – and she said, "Well, one will just ride with you and they'll keep their mouth shut. Just let them sit with you. Then I won't worry about you driving the next time." So John said, "I'll go with her." So he sat in the seat with me, and I took it off the hill. And he never told me anything. And I started driving on my own. When I learned to drive, I really wasn't old enough to get a driver's license.

I used to drive to school. You know I had a sick spell and I had to quit school for a while. When I went back, they kind of, I guess, petted me. I had a French class, and Mr. Dillon would – oh, that's when my voice was gone and he would give me something to write, my French, and I'd hand it in. Then I didn't have anything the next period. So I'd take the car and they'd let me come home. I'd just drive home. Women didn't drive much then.

Who were my best friends growing up? I had Ruth and C.V. Williams, twins, right here *[across the road from her house]*. C.V. couldn't climb, but I could. We lived in the tops of these trees out here. We'd get a sapling, climb up a young one, you know, and it would bend over. Then we'd, like monkeys, get the next one. My mother would call out and say, "Are you all in that?" – see, she couldn't see us – "Are you in those trees?" And as soon as we heard her call us, we hit the ground. "Are you up in those trees?" "No." We were not; we had already got down. She knew we'd been in the trees. But Ruth and C.V. and I and my brothers used to play ball out here in this road all the time. My mother had an onion patch over the fence. C.V. would climb over the fence and get him a big onion and a piece of cornbread and a handful of salt.

My dad worked at the prison and he walked across the hill to work. He would cross right down there across the creek and come up the hill, and we'd be out here playing ball. When we'd see him coming, we all ran to meet him. And he squatted down and held his arms out, and all the Williams and all the Rogers kids ran into his arms.

Fodderstack was a mine, and they had an old tipple where they let the cars down. I believe Fodderstack was the one where my dad got hurt. He was on top of one of the coal cars. The top was low in the mines, and he was laying on the top of the coal car, and it caught him between the top of the mine and the car. It knocked the breath out of him. They hollered for them to back it up. And he tried to tell them – he knew if they backed it up that it would double him up and break him all to pieces. But it knocked the breath out of him and he couldn't speak. So they backed it up and it broke I don't know how many ribs. They stuck in his lungs and let all the air out. Dr. Eblen took him to Knoxville to the hospital on the train. They didn't have ambulances. He said, "Bill, I thought that you'd be back next day, but I thought you'd be in a box." He had a lot of trouble. They didn't think he'd live. They said that sciatic rheumatism set up, and it would jerk his legs up to his chest. And all those ribs broken. They said you could hear him scream all over the hospital. But he lived. I was just a little bitty kid. My mother said I'd say, "I'm going to kill that old motor for hurting my daddy." They didn't think he would live.

He worked so hard through the week, and then Sunday was his only day off. He was a mine foreman up there where they had the coal mine. He had a bunch of prisoners. Bless his heart, he walked across. He would take the shortcut and go across by the reservoir and up to the prison. My mother would go out here on an icy cold morning and watch his light – he'd cross the creek and go up the bluff on the other side – to make sure he got there. She worried about him.

When war started, they needed help so bad they asked him – he was about 85 years old – would he come and sit on the guard shack. They would give him a room at the prison and give him his meals, and all he had to do was sit on there and hold the gun on it. He went. Velma was in Bristol teaching, and she cried. She couldn't stand the thought. I said, "Velma, if you saw how happy it made him. He felt like he was doing something worthwhile." And he was. I'd say, "Daddy, let me take you up to work." And he said, "No, I'm not letting you get up at four o'clock to go up there to take me. They're going to fix it just right for me." So I'd go get him lots of times after he got off from work, and he'd stay till bedtime, then he'd go back up there and sleep. When my brother John drowned, they came and told him. He was on the guard shack, and they told him. He never went back to work. That's when he quit.

My best friends growing up – well, of course, I had different ones. My high school friends, I had Jewel Scott from Lancing. And Evelyn Brasel and I were real good friends. They'd spend the night with me, and I'd spend the night with them. And Katie Heidel Peters was another one; we spent a lot of time together. And then Vera Beck was my good friend after we grew up. We've done a lot of traveling together. We'd go on tours and travel. We'd go to Florida and stay. We had some good times together. Louise Whitus was another. We used to double-date together. She was dating Frank Beene, and I was dating her cousin Doc Whaley.

We used to have parties. I know one time when the Slaughters lived over here where the Bedfords lived, Mrs. Slaughter had a party for something. It must have been Halloween because my brother Glenn dressed up like a woman. I've got his picture. He looks just like a woman. My mother had hair down about this long *[down to her hips]*. She saved the combings from her hair and had what they called a "switch." It was about a foot long. They fixed it up there at the top; she could pin that on and then do her hair any way she wanted to. It was her own hair, except straight, like a horse's tail. She pinned that on Glenn. They put a hat on him and fixed that hair. We took his picture. I believe it was Glenn and Thomas Slaughter sitting on the couch. Glenn looks just exactly like a woman. And Carl McGhee was fixed up like a farmer. He had on a straw hat. He and I were sitting together. I was a gypsy fortune teller, I believe.

But, anyway, we danced. Just the fox trot mostly or two-step. And we square-danced. I went to square-dances a lot. My mother never did care for us dancing at home and in homes like that – just as long as we didn't go to the beer joints – because she had always wanted to dance. She loved to dance. They used to square-dance. The Lehmans at that time were just friends and neighbors, and they would have what they called "parties," but then they'd square-dance. My grandmother thought my mother was going to the "party." She didn't much believe in "dances." They laughed about that a lot.

SCHOOLING

I attended elementary school in Petros, and Wartburg High School. I can't say what year I graduated. I had such a hard time. I had to stop, quit school, twice. See, I lost my voice once for a long time. They couldn't find out for forever what was wrong. I couldn't talk but above a whisper. They finally found a little tumor on my right vocal chord, and they stripped it. My voice was weak and it sounded funny at first. I was in high school. Then I had to stop another time. They put me to bed. I don't know what was wrong. Doctors never did know what was wrong with you, so they put you to bed to rest. They did that when I lost my voice. I was a senior, and it was near mid-term. Miss Ruth Winton and Velma, my sister, gave me my mid-term exams so I wouldn't miss my half-year of school – and me in bed. I took my exams in bed and got my half-year of credit. Miss Ruth said, "Next year you can go back the last half and finish and get your diploma." I said, "Yeah, and graduate with my brother Elbert? I'm not going back. He caught up with me and I'm not going. I don't want to graduate with Elbert!" She said, "Oh, Polly, you must! You must get that. It would be a shame if you just lacked half-a-year getting your diploma." I said, "I don't want it that bad." But with my mama and my sister – of course I went back. And I graduated with Elbert. What year was it? 1930?

I did go and take some college courses after that, but I didn't graduate. I didn't want to go to school. I took a beauty course for mine over at Knoxville at the Tennessee Beauty School. But Velma got her master's, and Hugh liked just writing his thesis getting his doctorate, and he wouldn't go back. He said he wasn't going to use it, and he was tired of going to school. I said, "Just to hang it on the wall, go back and get it." But he didn't. And of course Glenn graduated from medical school.

My daddy graduated from medical school. He was a dentist. But in those days people didn't use a toothbrush like they do now. They didn't make them, I guess. He said with some people the odor would be so bad that he would have been an alcoholic had he gone on. So he gave it up. He was a surveyor for awhile, and then he went to work as a mine foreman. He was an employee of the prison. There were mine prisoners. Of course, I don't know, they probably paid them – I know they did later on – for working. You know, a little bit. But his greatest desire was to see my brother Glenn start his dental practice. And he lived to see it. He gave him his leather case, and he had those pullers. And they had mercury for some reason; I guess in the fillings. Now they say it's dangerous, you know. I've seen my dad come home from work, his tooth would ache. He'd get those old pullers out and yank his own teeth without any anesthetic. Of course, my mother just went probably through grammar school. But she was smarter than a lot of people who had a college education. She had a lot of common sense.

SWEET MEMORIES

Roger Duncan was born in this house, my house. His parents were Elmer and Nelle Duncan, but he was our family baby. He's named after the Rogers. He couldn't say my mother's name – he called her "Oddie." He'd say, "Mama, I'm going down to Oddie's." And she'd say, "Oddie doesn't want to put up with you." Of course he went. My mother would be sewing, and she didn't like to be bothered when she was, you know, doing something serious like making a dress. She liked to be by herself and not have interruptions when she was sewing. So she'd sew with him down there until she'd kind of get nervous. He was afraid of the vacuum cleaner, so she'd just go get the vacuum and set it down in the floor, and he'd say, "Oddie, I better go home," and he'd go home.

We bought the house from Elmer and Nelle, and they moved to Jacksboro. Roger lives in Bristol. He's retired, but he's still playing the organ at the Methodist church. I believe he said he's been playing 50 years. We asked him to sing at my daddy's funeral – he sings beautifully – and he said, "If I can stand where I can't see the family, I will." We put him behind the flowers and he sang. We wouldn't ask him for Mama. My mother loved to hear him. He taught school, and he could tell the funniest things about those kids. He would just tickle you. The way he'd tell it, it was so funny. We loved to hear him. When my mother died, he wanted to play for the receiving, but we wouldn't ask him to sing because it was too hard for him. I told him I wanted him to sing at mine, but I'm going to let him go free because I know it would be hard for him.

I asked Polly if she remembered anything about Frederick and Augusta Engert, my great-grandparents. This led Polly to tell me about her stepfather, John Lehman. After Polly's father died, her mother married John Lehman. Here's their story, as related by Polly.

I don't remember Frederick and Augusta, but my mother did. I knew Bill and Gus Engert and the one at Oakdale. He lived on the other side of Oakdale, on Snow Hill Road. That's where their old home place was. I was trying to think what his name was. Charlie? I guess maybe Charlie. That's how come my mother to marry Mr. Lehman. Charlie died and my mother said, "Polly, I'd like to go to the funeral. They're going to bury him at Wartburg. Would you take me?" And I said, "Yeah." So after the funeral, we went down to the cemetery and we were walking up to the grave, and my mother said, "Polly, there's one of my old sweethearts 50 years ago. I wonder if he'll know me." He was standing with some other men, talking. And when we passed, he said, "Hello, Emma." And she said, "Hello, John." And they shook hands. I said, "I saw the love-light leap up in his eyes." She said, "Oh, Polly! You didn't do it!" I said, "Oh, yes. His eyes just sparkled when he saw you."

They were sweethearts 50 years earlier. When she was 16, she dated him. Then he went to Knoxville and got a job and went to work. He wrote her a letter – she lived down there at Mossy Grove on the farm – and she didn't get it. So she thought he didn't want to keep up the romance. So she didn't try to get in touch with him. And he thought she didn't want him, so he didn't write anymore. And they hadn't seen each other all that time. Well, my dad had been dead two or three years. I don't know how long his wife had been dead. But he had about seven kids, and she had six, grown and married. But, anyway, he went with Mrs. Engert the next day out to Wartburg to help settle up her funeral expenses, and he had her to bring him by here to see my mama. Velma, my sister, was at Oak Ridge and Mama had gone over there to stay with her during the winter. He'd catch the bus and go over there. And first thing you know they got married. So Mr. Charlie Engert's dying was the cause of them getting married.

MEMORIES OF PETROS UNITED METHODIST CHURCH

The first thing – that I don't remember myself, but my mother told me about – was when I was christened. I've been a member ever since. My mother said that our pastor was a young, single man. He had red hair and a real fair complexion. When he held me in his arms and put that cold water on my head, I screamed bloody murder and grabbed him by the hair with both hands and pulled it. She said his face was as red as his hair, it embarrassed him so. But, of course, that was when I was christened. Then I was baptized, I don't remember what year.

I have a lot of good memories. A lot of people have come and gone. I had a lot of good friends, and so many of them have passed away now, there's not too many left of our old members. My mother took us every Sunday. We had to be sick or something real bad if we missed going to church. I can see my mother today sitting at that end of her seat. I said I could not ever leave that church, because of her. She had a great influence on my life, and it still carries on. She was a good one. We all went. My daddy couldn't go often because he worked such long hours, but he went some.

We went to church in the old building. I started going in that. I can still remember that old church – I wish somebody had a picture. It was just one big room. I can't remember if we had a downstairs or not. Doesn't seem like we did. They tore it down when they built the new one. Brother Allison was our pastor. The prisoners did the labor. Most of it. We had the parsonage there, and we would have a full-time preacher. They rented the parsonage out when we didn't have a full-time preacher. Then they tore it down. I was always hoping they'd build another one back and we could get a full-time preacher. But they never did. We've got too few members.

I don't know who baptized me when I joined the church. I can't remember. But later Velma and I wanted to be immersed. So Brother Dail took us out to the Kellys' *[at Union]*, where that road goes around now, that old iron bridge, and baptized Velma and me and Mack Williams. That's where the Union Church – everybody – baptized in that hole. It was so clear. A beautiful place. I said, well, I'd had to have mine done over anyway for pulling the preacher's hair.

Polly remembers many of the people who went to church with her and her family.

Little Mrs. C.V. Williams and her family lived right here, close to my house. Ruth and C.V. – I grew up here with them. Their older sister was Hazel. She went to the Methodist church until she married and moved away. Mack and C.V., George, Walter – they all went. Mack and his family came along, and they went. And Mrs. Evans – Bob's mother – and Dorothy. And, of course, Bob Evans was there and Imogene. Her father, Gray Whitus, he came. And of course all the Whitus family. They were like the Rogers family – there was a whole passel of them. They're all gone, I believe, now. Miss Cora and Ed Whitus. Mrs. Annie Duncan and all of her children. Maudie Claiborne and Maudie's kids. They all scattered about. Mrs. Hattie Huskins Simpson. She was right on until the very last. And Mrs. Tucker – the Tuckers – Leona and Grace and Myrtle and Ruth, and then they had Eddie and Jasper. Myrtle Delaney – she and her husband lived somewhere else, and then after he died she came back to Petros. I don't know where they lived, whether it was up in LaFollette or in another state. Her husband was Charlie. Paralee Delaney – that was Myrtle's mother-in-law – she used to come up there. When they had their women's society, she belonged to that.

The ladies used to quilt in the back of the church, and Myrtle always said, "Whenever I die, I want you all to put a quilt up and have it back here quilting when they carry me in." I said, "Yeah, that would be something." Myrtle – she was a good person. She loved the little Methodist church better than anything. It was her whole life. So when she went to the nursing home, I'd go out and get her of the morning and bring her to the church and then take her back afterwards. I had to check her in and out. And everybody would be gathering for their lunch by then. I knew nearly all of them, and I'd just have to go from one table to the other and hug them all. By the time I got out of there, I was so depressed.

Then I got to thinking: I never asked her daughters if it was alright and what if I got her hurt. So I called Jeep, Myrtle's daughter. Jeep lived in Kentucky, and Mona, another daughter, lived in Kentucky or Ohio, I believe. But I called and talked to her. I said, "Jeep, I've never asked you if it's alright for me to go get her. What if I got her hurt or something?" She said, "Polly, she looks forward to that. That's the only thing she lives for. If you don't care, as long as she lives, if you'll go get her, I'll appreciate it. If she gets killed, that would be the way it's supposed to be. But that's her whole life, and if you don't mind I wish you'd just keep on." So I did until they took her to Rockwood and put her in the nursing home down there. I went to see her down there. But she went to all the Home Demonstration Club meetings. She took a part in that and a part in the church. She was a good person. Always when they changed the time, she and Dorothy Evans always got mixed up and they'd come an hour or two late or an hour or two early. She was a good person.

When I was young, we had the "Epworth League" – that was the young people's program – and we went on "possum hunts" they called it. Daddy said, "Why don't you say 'weeny roast' and be done cause you all don't hunt possums. You never bring one home. You go out and roast weenies and marshmallows and have a party." And we did. We hiked way up to the top of the mountain and built up a big fire. We had a good time.

In my mind I can still see Polly playing the organ every Sunday in church. She was slim and tall, with perfect posture. She always dressed stylishly, and she favored long earrings that dangled. Her snow-white hair was usually in an updo or she wore it flipped up on the ends, with never a hair out of place.

A young Polly modeling one of the dresses her mother made for her.

My mother always sewed our clothes. She even made dresses for me after I was grown. I hated to try on clothes. One time she made a skirt for me when I was at school. When I tried it on, it was just right. I asked her how did she make it fit me just perfect. She said, "I stood the broom up in the corner and fitted it on the broom handle."

I started getting gray when I was in high school. Mr. Williams that lived here, he was so funny. He said, "Polly, what caused your hair to be white was sitting in damp churches with cold feet listening to long sermons." I always think about him, what he said. My mother said, "Polly, put something on your hair. People will think I'm your sister instead of your mother." And I said, "I wouldn't care – I'd just as soon have you as my sister."

Really I don't know when I started playing at the Methodist church. I never thought about it. Flossie Bedford played, I guess, till she got married. Maybe it's after she got married that I started playing. But I don't know when it was. I played by ear for a long, long time. I had never had an organ lesson. I've had my organ forever, but I played the piano and you know you use the notes and everything – it's just a different touch. Years later, I started taking organ lessons from Harry Fritts. I had only taken lessons a few months, and Preacher Hancock out at Union Baptist Church wanted me to play. They had an organ just sitting there; nobody could play it. He said, "Polly, would you play?" I said, "I'm not ready. I've never had organ lessons. I just got started, and I haven't had too many lessons." And Harry said, "Polly, you are ready. You have a natural ear for music, and it's no problem for you. You just don't have any self-confidence. You are ready. Go ahead and play."

Tom Fritts was the music director out there, and his wife Glenda played the piano. When they asked me, at first I wouldn't do it because I said I wasn't ready. Glenda said, "I don't care if you just hit a note now and then." I said, "I don't do things like that. I want to do it right if I do it." But I told the preacher, "I'll play till you find somebody better." And every time I'd ask him had he found anybody, he'd say, "We've got who we want." So I played four years out there at Union Baptist

Church. They've been trying to get me to come back and play again, but I won't, because I'm out of practice. I don't play anymore.

Velma had more music than I. But she had to dig for hers. Harry Fritts said I had an ear for music. I had a natural talent. I could hear a song and then play it. Growing up, Velma and I had a piano, and before that my mother had one of the old-timey organs – like we've got over at the church – a pedal. That was my mother's. She could play. She played the guitar too. But then when I got big enough, she thought I was old enough and had sense enough for my music lesson, I took from Mrs. Aileen Slaughter a little while. And I took from Laura Ford a little while. And then I took one year in school. The principal's wife – I can't remember her name – taught me. And then I took a year at Wartburg. I got a certificate for music.

Polly also sang.

Mavis Carr, Patsy Bonifacius, Peg Comer and I sang together at church. I sang tenor for awhile, and then soprano. I can't sing anymore.

When I asked her what her favorite songs are, Polly replied...

"Amazing Grace" is one. And "It Is Well With My Soul." I love that.

Polly was the secretary and treasurer of the church. After she read her secretary/treasurer's report each Sunday, she always asked if anybody had celebrated a birthday during the week. If you had, you got to walk up front and put your birthday collection in a special box shaped like a church while the congregation sang "Happy Birthday." One man, Mr. Morelock, always counted out pennies for each of his years.

I took over when Lucy Patrick got pregnant with Pat. She was the secretary. Whenever she got pregnant, that's when she quit. I said I resigned a dozen times. I said, "How do you resign a job?" They said, "You just have to die and leave it." And I just about did. I don't know when I quit; when it got so I couldn't go to church anymore.

You know, we used to have so many. We had a church full. All those people that used to live at the prison, most of them were Methodists. I believe there were more Methodists than there were Baptists. I was sitting in the car the other day, and I started writing down a list of all the people I could remember. The Stranges. The Acuffs. The Rosses. The Boones. The Records. The Stockards. The Kellys. All the

Longs – Riley Long and Ross Long were brothers. The Fusons. Mr. Morelock – he kept the flowers blooming. He was always doing something. You know where the rock wall is, there where you park at church? He had scarlet sage planted down there. Mr. and Mrs. E. B. Douglass lived at the prison; she was my Sunday School teacher. I remember some Cooks. And Gene Woodward went. And Grandmother Bardill. Susie and Paul Waldrop.

I had to take Shawnie Waldrop home with me every Sunday. She cried if she didn't get to go. She'd say, "I'm going home with you." I'd say, "Ok." And she'd say, "Daddy, can I go home with Polly?" He'd say, "No. Polly's tired of taking you every Sunday. You go home. They don't want to put up with you." And she started crying. I said, "Let her go." We went out to eat every Sunday. We took her everywhere. I got her Christmas presents and birthday presents. One time, years later, Susie got my name at the Christmas party. We drew names and she got my name. She got me a bottle of Elizabeth Taylor's perfume. It was $25 a bottle, and that was too much. It's more than that now. I said, "Susie, I can't take it – this is too much." She said, "All the gifts you bought my kids, this is the first time I've got to try to even get anything for you." I said, "You take it back." And she said, "I won't do it."

Do you remember when we had a Christmas program one night and we couldn't get a Santa Claus? We finally got Buster Hobbs to be the Santa Claus. He drank every once in a while. So it started snowing, and he came up the steps stomping, making the awfulest noise – they didn't know he was drinking – and he said, "Ho, ho, ho! It was snowing like hell when I left the North Pole." In church! The last time he was down here – he lived up North and that's where he died – he came in the post office and we were laughing about that. We had never forgotten that. He said, "They ought to have known better than to ask me to be Santa Claus when I was drinking." I said, "Well, nobody knew you were drinking that night."

Verna Kelly used to sing proper, you know opera-like, at church. My brother Elbert and Charles Alderson were sitting back there, and of course they were giggling amongst themselves. But she saw them and she told my mother that they were making fun of her singing. Elbert said, "We didn't even hear her; we were just talking amongst ourselves and laughing, Mama. We weren't making fun of her." "Well," my mother said, "you had no business talking and laughing in church." My mama got after Elbert anyway for it.

Maggie Patrick. And then Paul Patrick; he was the old bachelor, Oscar's brother. He gave me money every time he got his check I reckon for a long, long time. He tithed. I'd put tithes in for him. He came sometimes, but he was not a regular member. But he was a faithful one to pay. So I figured that we'd count him because he gave.

Ronnie Jackson – he's still a member. He goes to church in Oak Ridge, but he's never moved his membership. He lived with us, you know, until he got married.

There's N.D. Booher and Mrs. Booher. They lived across the street from the church. He was the depot agent when we had a train coming in. He wouldn't move his membership. He was 90-some-years-old when he died, and he had just moved it a year or two before he died. He would write me, and he sent me a picture of him out in his garden plowing with a push plow. He was 90 years old. That was one of our older ones. They didn't have any children.

Mr. Booher was sitting on the back seat when my mother took me out for misbehaving in church, and he said, "Mrs. Rogers, when you took that little girl out for misbehaving, I started to say, 'Spank her.'" And he told his wife, said, "I believe she did, and I'd have hated it." My mama said, "I'll tell you one thing: If you see me take one out for misbehaving, they're going to get spanked." Well, I started acting up again and she had to take me out. She always told it on me – she always took one out ONE time and it broke them. But me – she had to take me twice the same day. I was a stubborn one. A little shingle had blown off the church, and she picked it up. When she came back in, I was sitting in her lap. She put my dress over it, pulled it over it. I reached down and got it and broke it over my knee and threw it down in the floor. She said, "Young lady," – after she got me home – "that wouldn't have kept you from getting a spanking, throwing it down in the floor. They've got other shingles out there that I could use."

After Mrs. Booher died, Mr. Booher moved to Oneida. He was in charge of the oil company over there. He remarried, and they had two sons. He was turning somersaults on the bed playing with them, and he went through the plate glass window feet first.

Mrs. Chester and daughter. She was a widow, and she had a daughter, Reba. Reba married George Dagley. They both taught school. Then they moved to Wartburg. She played the organ at the Methodist church for a long time. She was the first one I remember playing the organ.

A family moved here from Nashville, and he worked in the office at the prison. They had a big family. I can't remember the parents going to our church, but all the kids went. They had three boys and two girls. I played with the girls. They had long hair. We'd get in a fight and they'd whip me because I was just one. I had short hair, but they had long hair. But two of them on one – they'd always win – and I'd go home crying, I guess. But John, my brother, said, "I'm going to show you how to whip them girls." So he'd sit on the sidelines, and he'd say, "Pull their hair!" And I'd get this one, and then the other one. And I'd send them home crying. They quit fighting me. But they gave me lice. Their mother was from Nashville and a city woman. She didn't know what they were. I played with them, and every time I'd come in, they'd come out and call me out to play. My mother would say, "You know what happens." When I'd come back in, my mother would look at my head and comb it with a fine-tooth comb and wash it and everything. And I'd yell bloody murder. She said, "If you're going to play with them, you're going to have to go through this every time." I said, "Why don't you tell their mother that they've got lice?" But she didn't want to do that. Then they moved back to Nashville.

Buster Watkins. He was Mrs. Patsy Bonifacius' nephew. His mother was Mrs. Bonifacius' sister, Hassie Watkins.

Buster was a young man when he died, and his funeral was held in the Methodist church. In the days before his death, Buster had placed wood and coal in the stove at the church in preparation for Sunday morning services. Longtime church members reminisce that Buster made the fire that heated the church house for his own funeral.

And remember Viley Phillips and her two little granddaughters, Margie and Ivory? They could sing like birds. I remember them singing a Christmas song that was so pretty. They could sing.

Mr. and Mrs. Simpson and Walter Lee ("Nub"), Mr. Simpson's son. Walter Lee on Halloween – Lug Hammonds, you know, lived down there at the foot of the hill. They had their toilet across the creek, down from the graveyard hill, right down at the foot of the hill. A bunch of boys used to turn over toilets on Halloween. They said, "Let's go turn over Lug's toilet." They went and turned it over earlier, and then they waited until it got dark and they got up on the hill, and they said, "Now we'll count three, we'll all run down the hill." They dropped back and let Walter Lee go, and he didn't know it, and he fell in the pit. When he went home – Miss Hattie had a rain barrel out there. She made him get in the rain barrel and wash before she'd let him get in the house.

Levi Brasel. Mr. Levi Brasel was Miss Ruth Winton's grandfather. He lived at Union until after his wife died and he came and lived with Mrs. Dora Winton and Ruth and Frank. He went to the Baptist church, and he was teaching a Sunday School class. He was a smart old man. Because he belonged at Union – and, see,

Union was the one that really helped form this Baptist church down here – they put him out as a Sunday School teacher because he didn't belong to their Baptist church. They wouldn't let him take communion with them. He belonged to the Baptist church at Union. He came up to our church and taught. Mr. Brasel – I used to go get him sometimes when he didn't have a ride. My grandma got in the car up at the church one time. We were taking Mr. Brasel home, and he had a big old heavy overcoat on. She'd sat down on his overcoat, and he couldn't move. He said, "Miss Bardill, you're sitting on my tail!" He was a good old man. He was going to buy me a barrel of candy. Always, he was going to. And I looked for it. I believed it then. You know, I was little. I thought he would really get me a barrel of candy. But he never did.

Judson Taylor *(the Baptist preacher)* and his wife taught school up here. He asked my sister Velma to go somewhere with them to a teacher's meeting. She told him, "I'm afraid you won't let me eat with you. You'd make me sit at a different table." He said, "Well, we might consider letting you sit with us."

Herbert Lowe. He came every Sunday to the Methodist church. On his birthday, his kids always gave us money. Nellie and Juanita and Tiny Langley came. Minnie Hatfield. Minnie and I were real close.

I was trying to think last night of the different preachers that I could remember. Reagan Allison and Charlie Bray. Austin White. And Chambers – he was that little Polish guy. He was a prisoner of war, by the Germans, during the war. He could play the piano. He played by ear, I guess. He could play "Dark Town Strutters Ball" – he didn't play just the religious ones. I mean, he played them! And his feet wouldn't touch the floor. He'd swing his feet. He was short.

One preacher we had, the first time he came, he didn't have a car. Didn't have a way. He said if somebody would meet the bus at Oliver Springs, he'd preach that night. So Doc was here, and he and Velma and I went to get him. Velma had a little Chevrolet coupe. A one-seater. So the four of us rode in that. We picked him up there at Oliver Springs at the bus station. Of course we took him up to our house. Emmy always cooked dinner, and then we ate leftovers for supper on Sunday night. She always had a lot left over.

That Sunday she had chili. So he ate chili. And we started to church. I was driving the car, and we had a flat tire. So we had to walk. Doc and I went down the short way, and the rest of them – my daddy and Emmy and the preacher and some of the other kids – went around the road because it was easier walking. Anyway, those gravels – they had gravel roads, it wasn't black-top then, it was gravel – he was just rolling and rolling up on them. They were afraid he was going to fall down. And he rolled on one, and he let a big one. He said, "Uuuuhhhhmmmm," and started clearing his throat. Emmy thought that Doc and I were behind them, but we didn't go that way. We had gone down the other way. And of course we missed it.

The next morning, Mama came to wake me up, and she was dying laughing about it. She said, "Where were you and Doc?" I said, "We went the short cut. We missed it." And that disappointed her, because she was hoping we were behind them. My mother called him "Brother Thunder" the rest of the time he was there. Yes. "Brother Thunder." And she told Flossie and Slim Halburnt. Slim was funny. She was telling them about it, and Slim never did get over that. He said, "Emmy, when have you seen Brother Thunder?" The rest of the time he was "Brother Thunder" with us. Oh, law.

We had a Perkins. He was one a long, long time ago. Preacher Perkins. My aunt was down here with her son Ernest, and my mother had a little dog. Its name was Trixie. Ernest couldn't talk plain. He said, "Twixie, you look just like Preacher Perkins." In a few minutes, they looked out and saw Preacher Perkins coming. They were scared to death that he would tell him. So they told him, of course, not to. But he was in the room with the preacher, and he started to tell him. Aunt Dora was standing in the room back here where she could see her son but not the preacher. He'd start it, and she'd shake her head. And then he'd look in there at her, and he'd say, "I ain't going to tell it." I don't know if he ever told it or not. Preacher Perkins.

Ernest Howard – I saw his kids the other night, and they all knew me.

We had Brother Dail two or three different times. He was good. My mother asked for him back. She's the one that got him back. I always enjoyed Brother Dail when he was our pastor.

I loved the Easter Sunrise service and the breakfasts. Really it was more thrilling, it was more sacred, than Christmas. And I loved our little Christmas program.

We had a Christmas program one time. Do you remember when they made the little white milk cans and covered them, made them white, with white crepe paper? We wrapped the limbs of just a plain tree – had a white Christmas tree. And we had those little cans; they weren't on the tree, but they had them up there. They were wrapped. They had a hole in them and they put money in them. I don't know what we used it for – some special offering. Anyway, I was Mary and Lawrence Duncan was Joseph, and we had a big doll in the cradle for the Baby Jesus. One of the boys playing a wise man couldn't talk plain. He had a speech impediment. He said,

"Christ of lowly birf" – he didn't say birth; he said birf – "come down to rule the earth." And what else did he say? I've about forgotten. I thought of that again today. "Christ of lowly birth; come to rule the earth." And he said, "No, that's not right. Come to rule the roof. Christ of roly bruth come to rule the roof." And then he said, "No, that ain't right." Then he started over, and he said it the same way. And by that time, I was – Emmy said that I ruined the program for laughing. I couldn't help it. I was shaking. I had my head down. I wouldn't look at Lawrence. Of course Lawrence was standing there, never moved a muscle. He didn't. And I was sitting there laughing. I said, "Well, they could have thought I was crying." But she always told me I ruined the program.

Wanda Lauderback – do you remember the Lauderbacks? Wanda married a Snodgrass and moved to Kingsport. My mother and Mrs. Lauderback were real good friends. They used to come over here a lot. Every time they'd come over to the house, we'd all get together and sing and have a good time. She and my mother hiked to the tower with a whole bunch of us from the church.

My brother Glenn and Harmon Lauderback were buddies. Lynn Myer Lauderback was the baby and was spoiled. They lived on Georgia Row, and Mrs. Lauderback would walk across the hill to our house. When she would walk over, she'd bring Lynn Myer – the others would be in school – and every time he came to my mother's, he'd say, "Mama, I want something to eat." He was always hungry, cause Emmy always had goodies, you know. His mother had said, "Lynn Myer, if you go over to Mrs. Rogers' and ask for anything to eat today, I'm going to whip you." So he got along fine for ever so long, and then he said, "Oh, my stomach feels in the need of something to eat" – which was just as good as saying feed him. That tickled my mother to death. She got him something to eat. He didn't really ask for food; that was his way of getting around it.

After they moved to Kingsport, Mr. Lauderback died and Harmon died. Wanda wrote me for the longest time. When Lynn Myer died – he was young – he was a lawyer up in Kingsport– and I saw it in the paper, I called her. And Klyne – I saw something about him the other day in the paper. He's a lawyer too.

The Fusons lived in a house where you go in the gates up there at the prison, close to where the old church was. We set a "dumb supper" up there one night. A dumb supper is where you do everything backwards. You turn out the lights and you do everything backwards. You don't turn around. And then when you get the table set, you sit down and the man you're going to marry will come and sit down in the seat. You'd set a place for him, and he'll come and sit down at the table when you get it fixed. So we did it one night up at the Fusons. The moon was shining bright, and I looked out the window and somebody was watching us. He had on a white shirt so it couldn't have been a prisoner. They lived right there next to the prison. Somebody found it out; somebody was watching us. Scared the girls to death. They thought it was a prisoner. I said, "It wasn't a prisoner cause they don't wear white shirts." This one had on a white shirt. He was leaning up against that building, watching us – Kate and Ann Rice and the Fusons and probably Wanda Lauderback – through the window.

I was trying to think. We used to have picnics. They quit having the picnics anymore. We would go out to Crossville to the park. Oh, I loved them there. And, of course, out here at Frozen Head a lot. Seems to me like the church went up to Caryville once to Cove Lake Park. And we used to have dinners down in the basement of the church. I used to fix barbeque chicken for church dinners – that was my specialty – and usually I'd make a cake of some kind. I don't cook anymore. My favorite food, well, I guess I eat macaroni and cheese an awful lot. It's one of my favorite ones. And I like pound cake. Minnie Hatfield used to make them for me. That was her specialty. She'd bake that.

LIFE IN PETROS

I was never afraid of living so close to the prison. So many people over at Knoxville or around will ask you, "Aren't you scared?" And I'd say, "No. When they get out here, they're trying to get *out* of Petros. They're not hanging around here." I never have been afraid.

I remember a lot of prison escapes. I remember I was sitting there at the church when one came across, passed the window, and went by Lucy Patrick's. He saw it was the end of the road so he came back and went down to Mrs. Portwood's. He got some clothes off the line and he went in the outdoor toilet there. But they caught him before he got very far away. When the whistle used to blow *[to alert townspeople that a prisoner had escaped]*, it was the lonesomest sounding thing. I hated it.

I remember when that one got away and went down through Rock Bridge Road down there on the Harriman Highway and raped that woman. That was the last electrocution that Tennessee had until just lately. They used to go down Black Creek. I worried about Mrs. Bowles when she lived down there; they had the garage. I'd take her to the show. We'd go to the drive-in, and I'd always wait till I knew she was in because she was right on that creek and they came down that Black Creek a lot. And it was bushes where you couldn't see too good. I always waited until she got in her house before I went on. They used to – they trained the dogs, and they'd come across through here a lot of times with the prisoners. They'd let one prisoner go on ahead, and he'd climb a tree and get out of the way, then here they'd come with the dogs to trail him. That was their favorite one up there.

Did Petros have telephones when Polly was growing up?

Mrs. Quisenberry had the only telephone in the drugstore down there, and everybody had to go down there and make their telephone calls. I remember when Nina (our brother Elbert's wife) died, they called there. Velma and I were down at Oakdale spending the night with the McCartys, and they called down there. Mrs. Quisenberry called. She had got the message that Nina had died. Later, when we got a phone, I always tried not to stay on it. I never did like real long conversations anyway. I can't talk like that on the telephone. I just say what I usually need to say and that's it.

A long time ago Petros had a mayor. I've heard my mother talk about it. It was incorporated. Mose Bunch had the post office there, I guess, where Lawrence Duncan's store was. And then they had that bank building across the road. Probably Mose Bunch might have been mayor. I don't know.

Early doctoring and remedies . . .

Well, for doctoring, they used to give castor oil. Especially to women before they had babies, you know, when they were in labor. To hurry it up, they'd give them castor oil. I'd heard of that. I never had any kids, so I don't know. But I've seen my daddy come in and he'd be feeling bad. He'd pick up the castor oil bottle and just turn it up and drink it out of the bottle. I couldn't stand it. My mother used to give us worm medicine. Kids used to get wormy I reckon. "Vermifuge" I believe they called it. Oh, goodness, I couldn't stand that stuff. When my mother would give it, she'd show me pictures in the fire or something to get my mind off of it. My mother used a lot of home remedies. I think they are better. I think doctors kill more people than the diseases do.

Miss Hattie coughed so hard at church sometimes she was embarrassed and was about to quit coming. My mother said, "Miss Hattie, I could fix you some cough medicine if you will take it." She said, "Oh, Mrs. Lehman, I'd take about anything to stop this." So Emmy sent me to the liquor store, and I got some apple brandy. The doctor had got that for me one time, with rock candy. And I believe she put maybe lemon juice. What else did she put in it? Sometimes they put glycerine in it. Mix this all up and just take it by the spoonful, and it'll stop you from coughing. I had pleurisy and I was so sore I couldn't turn over in bed. My daddy and my brother John went to Oneida, Scott County, and got some homemade apple brandy, and they fixed it up with rock candy and all that sort of stuff and gave it to me. And, you know, it stopped that. That was a good home remedy. But Miss Hattie, when she'd get nearly out, I'd say, "Let me know and I'll go back to the liquor store." She always called Emmy when anything got wrong with her. She said Emmy was her doctor. When Emmy died, she said, "I've lost my doctor."

POLITICS

My daddy was a strong Democrat. He was very serious about it. He probably voted me as soon as I was old enough. Oh, yes. He'd fight you. My mother was worse than he was. She would fight you over politics. She was really into politics. She loved it. My daddy never missed an election. They didn't have to work on that day, and he'd go down to the polls and they had him as a watcher. Oh, they used to be so crooked. They had him watching. A watchman. You know, one woman in town would always hold out for a bottle of whiskey. She'd sell her vote for whiskey. She'd wait to the last to see who'd give her the most before she'd vote. One family had a dog and they voted him. I know one time it was so crooked.

The Democrats were two factions. They were against each other. They appointed my daddy as a watcher to watch to see that they didn't cheat. So my dad did. My mother cooked dinner up at her house and had them bring the workers up there for lunch. All of them got in the car and went up there, so Dad just climbed in the car too. Em tried to get Dad to come and eat. Dad said, "No. I didn't come to eat. I came to watch to see that everything is all right." He wouldn't eat, but he watched that ballot box. They took the ballot box and sat it down, and Dad sat down and watched.

I don't remember the first President that I voted for. The one that sticks close to me was Roosevelt, but I know I voted a long time before Roosevelt. But he was one of my favorite ones. He's the one that started Social Security. I saw him twice. I saw him down at Oakdale when he came through. I was working in Oakdale at the post office. The post master was in the hospital, and they called me from Knoxville and asked me to go over there and work in his place, and I did. He came through on the train. He didn't stay but a few minutes in Oakdale, but I saw him. When I was going to beauty school in Knoxville, he came down the street. They had a parade, and he was in this car with the top down. He was waving at everybody, and I was upstairs on I guess the second floor. He had his hat off, and he was waving at everybody. Oh, I saw him three times. I saw him down in Miami. He made a speech at the park downtown in Miami, and I was there. So I really saw him three times.

MARRIAGES AND TRAGEDIES

One of the sweetest but saddest chapters in Polly's life became known to a younger generation on June 5, 2000, when Zach Wamp, U.S. Congressman from Tennessee, came to Wartburg to present Polly, the widow of a World War II hero, with the medals her husband earned 55 years earlier. This is the story of Polly and Milton ("Doc") Whaley.

Doc lived at Oakdale. He was going to school there, and I was going to school at Wartburg. We had an Epworth League at church, and we went on "possum hunts" they called it. Daddy said, "You know, honey, you never bring a possum home. Why don't you just say you're going on a weeny roast?" We'd take marshmallows and weenies and everything. We'd go way up in the woods and build up a big fire. Doc was visiting. He was a cousin of the Whitus and the Koontz families. His mother, Clara, was a sister to George Koontz and Cora Whitus. He was visiting Tom Whitus, and Tom brought him on that. Of course we, that group, didn't date; we were just good friends. We might pair up, but we were not dating or anything. But he told Tom when he saw me, "I think introductions are in order." And Tom introduced him, and then I went with him and that started it.

When he graduated from Oakdale, he had an older sister in Chicago and as they'd graduate down here, she'd take them up there and find them a job. He worked for awhile, and then he went to college. He took ROTC in school, and whenever he graduated, he was in the service automatically for at least two years.

We were engaged to get married in June. I wanted a church wedding. He wanted me to come up there for that Thanksgiving *[1940]*. He said, "Would you come up?" His mother and his brothers had an apartment up there. He was at Fort Sheridan, and Fort Sheridan wasn't very far from Chicago and he could run down there. My daddy was old-fashioned, and even though we were engaged, he didn't want me to go up to

Milton ("Doc") Whaley, Polly's first love.

Chicago by myself, because Chicago was where I would have had to stay. That's where the apartment was. So Dad said, "I'd just rather you didn't go." So I obeyed my father. I sent Doc a message and told him I couldn't come. Hugh, my brother, had a girlfriend in Cookeville where he was going to school. I didn't like her. She told Hugh that she was coming up here for Thanksgiving. She invited herself. So I said, "Ok. If she's coming here, I'm going to Chicago." So my daddy agreed. I sent Doc a wire, and I said meet a certain train, I'll be on it. And I did. I was just going to stay through the Thanksgiving holidays. I just took enough clothes to spend that long.

But Doc talked me into getting married. He knew he was going to go overseas, I think. He talked me into getting married then. I wired my mama. I told her I was getting married and could anybody come to the wedding. Of course nobody could come to Chicago on that short notice. My mama wired me back. She said, "Polly, if you're going to get married, you have to have a suit, a dress, something to wear. I'm wiring you some money to buy you an outfit." And she did. I wore a royal blue velvet dress and hat. I don't think it had a brim. It was just kind of fancy for a wedding, more than just an everyday hat. That was my favorite color. Royal blue was my color. We were married in Christian Church – a huge, beautiful church – in the sanctuary. We had Joe Hall and Alene (Doc's sister). And Lewis Kittrell, I believe his name was, from Oakdale was up there working, and he went. We just had a small wedding.

Until we got our license up there, and they asked, "Place of birth?" and he said, "Petros, Tennessee," I didn't know Doc was born in Petros too. I said, "You weren't born in Petros," and he said, "Yes, I was." He was born right across the street from where Bill Murray lives today. So we got married on Thanksgiving 1940 at this church. It was so cold up there. He made me go out and buy galoshes, the worst thing. I hated galoshes. But everybody wore them up there, that snow.

Polly and Doc Whaley a few days after their wedding in Chicago, Thanksgiving 1940.

When I went up there, he got me a place to stay there in the same apartment building where his mother and brothers lived. I was just going to stay over the Thanksgiving holiday. I didn't plan to stay. Then after we got married, they gave us a house on the base. A great big old beautiful brick home. Huge. Right on the lake. You could walk down to the end of the block to the lake. In the wintertime with it frozen over – the lake would freeze over – it was so cold. I hated Chicago because I froze to death.

Doc Whaley.

But I kept writing, saying, "Mama, send me this, that or the other." And Doc said, "You know Emmy's going to get tired of mailing you stuff. Why don't you just run down there and get what you need?" And I did. I ran down here, and I stayed two weeks. A new bride. They all told him – his buddies at Fort Sheridan – that I'd gone AWOL and I wasn't coming back. And he got to believing it, you know. I was up at Miss Rice's – my good friend. When I came home, they were giving me showers and parties and everything, and I was having a good time and was in no hurry to go back. He sent me a wire and said, "I suggest you get the train out tomorrow" – a certain time – "and I'll be in Chicago the next day to meet you." I sent him a wire back. I said, "Sorry I can't make it that day. I'll make it the next day." So he met me at the station. He wrote my mama a card. He said, "Mom, I thought she wasn't coming back." And in about two weeks he got his orders to go overseas. I said, "Had I known you were going to leave, I would not have gone home." He said, "Oh, yeah, you would have. You were so homesick that nothing could have kept you from that."

We came home for Easter *[1941]*. Came home on a Saturday. Then we were here for Easter Sunday. And Monday he got on a train at Oakdale and left. I was standing at the depot. When he went through the tunnel, he was still standing waving goodbye to me, standing on the steps of the train on the back. It was just full of soldiers. Our trooper – Gary Snow – well, his mother and father, I found out later they were there. They were good friends of Doc's and neighbors, and they were there to see him off too. But they felt so sorry for me, they didn't say anything. They didn't bother him. But my mother and I took him to the train. And that's the last I ever saw him.

I know Kyle McCarty was the railroad detective. He was just 16 when my mother got married. They were buddies. They lived side-by-side. He was a railroad detective in Oakdale, and they lived up there on the hill. He took my mother and me up there in his car. He said, "Polly, you're in no shape to drive home." I shouldn't tell you what he gave me. He fixed me an apricot brandy and made me drink that straight. And you know, I never felt anything. Nothing. I waited awhile to see if I was going to get drunk, but I didn't feel anything so I came on home.

Doc was sent to the Province of Bataan, Philippines. Polly planned to join him there after a year, but on December 7, 1941, the Japanese bombed Pearl Harbor and then invaded the Philippines. U.S. and Filipino soldiers defended Bataan for three months before surrendering on April 9, 1942. Doc was taken prisoner by the Japanese. He survived the infamous Bataan Death March, a forced march to the prison camps during which American and Filipino prisoners were beaten, starved or murdered by Japanese troops.

I had three years – he was a prisoner of war – that I didn't know if he was living or dead. But I felt him near. I knew when he died. All at once I couldn't reach him. They kept saying, "You might as well give up, that he's . . ." But I said, "No! He's not gone. He's alive. I can feel him." But when I had that feeling that I couldn't reach him anymore, I knew he was gone.

Doc was eventually sent to Bilibid Prison in Manila, and on December 13, 1944, he was placed onboard the Oryoku Maru. Destination: Japan. The ship was not marked as a POW ship, and American forces bombed the ship. Doc survived this bombing, but was put on another ship.

He was a prisoner. They were taking the prisoners to Japan. The last boat that started to Japan was not marked as a prisoner of war ship. Our boys flew over and bombed the ship and sank it. But a lot of them survived that. They swam to shore. And he did. He had a friend on there, Bill Miner. Doc graduated from Knox College in Galesburg, Illinois, and his buddy, Bill, had graduated there too. They were together all the time. But the other man (Bill) came back. He wrote me a letter and told me all about it. He said that most of their prisoner-of-war time, they were together. They'd move them from one place to the other, but he said there were about two months out of that three years they were not together. He said that Doc swam to shore, that both of them did. And the next day they put them on another ship and started to Japan again with them. And our boys came back and bombed it again. And he was on the side where the bomb hit.

Doc died January 9, 1945.

Bill Miner told me that Doc died from a concussion, that there wasn't a mark on his body. But I couldn't believe that. A bomb hit a ship. He just wanted to make me feel good.

Doc was a good friend of Bill's parents too. His sisters also went to that school and they were good friends. All during the war, Mr. and Mrs. Miner wrote me every time they could get any news at all. I got telegrams and everything. They kept me informed. But Bill came back. He lived in Bloomington, Indiana. An article in the *Knoxville News Sentinel* awhile back said Bill Miner's son, Lewis Miner, had written a book about his father's experience while he was a prisoner of war and all that. And I said, "That's Doc's friend – his father." He wanted to write a book about it for his grandchildren so they would have something and know what went on and everything.

The book, researched and edited by Bill Miner's son, Lewis A. Miner, is entitled SURRENDER ON CEBU: A POW'S DIARY - WWII. *It contains a copy of the diary – some accounts written down on Japanese toilet paper – Bill Miner kept while he was a Japanese Prisoner of War. Polly's husband, Capt. Milton (Doc) Whaley, is mentioned on pages 137, 143, 145, 178-179, and 187 of the book.*

Bill Miner was rescued while in Hoten POW Camp at Mukden, Manchuria, by the Russian forces on August 18, 1945, seven months after Doc Whaley died. He had survived six different POW camps and six Japanese "Hell Ships." He weighed 60 pounds when he was rescued. Upon returning home, he finished his Ph.D. in history at Indiana University. He retired in 1980 as Professor of History, Assistant Dean of Students and Director of Veterans Services at Eastern Illinois University at Charleston, Illinois. He died in 1998 at the age of 83.

I was going to a doctor at Sunbright, taking some shots. I was out there when they got the telegram from the War Department that Doc was dead. We had a Preacher Bray from Kingsport. He brought Velma, my sister, out there, and they brought – they opened the telegram because they knew, you know, had an idea. The doctor wasn't in, but his wife was there. They told her. They didn't tell me. I said, "What are you doing out here?" They said, "We were riding around, and we just thought we'd check up on you." They didn't tell me. And so they told his wife, and she told the doctor when he came in.

When the doctor called me in there, first thing he did was ram a needle in my arm, and I didn't know what it was all about. I don't know what he gave me, but anyway I couldn't cry for three days. I thought I would die. Don't ever let them give you a shot. You might as well – you're going to have to know it and feel it. Sometimes it's better to get it out than it is to wait three days. I'd feel like I was going to die inside. I couldn't let it out. I just kept everything bottled up. It's better to let it out if you can. I said, well, I didn't explode but I felt like I was going to sometime.

Doc's the – the love was the light of my life. I said you can love more than once, but it's not the same, is it? He was a good man. He was smart. His sister Alene and her husband – she was always so good to me. She lived in Chicago, then she moved down here close to where the cemetery is in Oakdale. She and I put up Doc's marker. We couldn't get a man – none of them had time for us – and I got one of those markers from the Veterans, and she and I put it up. I never mixed concrete before, but I know how now, and it's still standing after all these years. It still looks good. So I should get me a union card and go to work in concrete.

I asked Polly what it was like for her after she found out that her husband hadn't survived.

That he had died? Well, I'll tell you I was on the road all the time. The people wondered why I went all the time.

There's the medals that Zach Wamp presented to me after 55 years.

Congressman Wamp formally presented the Purple Heart, Prisoner of War, American Defense, Asiatic Pacific Campaign, Victory, Rifle and World War II medals to Polly. After Doc's death, Polly had received only his Purple Heart – and that was through

On June 5, 2000, U.S. Congressman Zach Wamp presented Polly with six medals her husband, Capt. Whaley, earned in World War II.

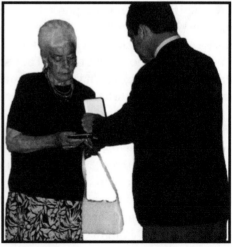

the mail. All those years, she never looked at it, but her family did. She is still visibly upset that it was mailed to her.

I didn't get his body back. It's in Subic Bay in the Philippines. But I have a marker in the family cemetery the other side of Oakdale, there on Snow Hill Road, and I take flowers there. I hate to go up there by myself because it's lonesome. Well, it's – I just don't like to go by myself. That was my first love.

Why was he called "Doc"?

Because his grandfather, Dr. William Koontz, was a doctor. They said he looked so much like his grandfather, they got to calling him "Doc." His name was Milton Whaley.

When I commented that Polly has lived quite a life . . .

Honey, I have really. It's sort of sad. And then I had Gene Woodward. We were married. Doc and I were married five months – we had five months together. But Gene and I had 13 years. He died in 1964. He committed suicide. Some of them say, "Why don't you marry Bill Murray?" I told them I didn't want to marry anymore. I said, "I think I'm bad luck for a man." I had such bad luck, I didn't want to try. I don't know what else could happen, but I didn't want to get married anymore. I'll just be an old "widdy."

I married Gene in 1950. Married Doc in 1940. There was 10 years apart. But, see, I didn't know whether Doc was living or dead for so long. They just had him Missing in Action. But I knew when he died. I always had that closeness. As long as he was living, I felt near to him. And then when he was dead, all at once I had that feeling I couldn't reach him. My mother said, "Polly, you're going to have to face it. You know you don't believe he's coming back." And I said, "He *is* coming back. I know he is. I know he's still alive." But then all at once, I felt that he wasn't close anymore, and I knew he was gone.

Doc and I were going to get married in the little Methodist church in Petros in June. And then I went up there at Thanksgiving, just for Thanksgiving. He knew he was going overseas. He knew all of that. I think he knew that they were going to have a war, but he never told me. So we had planned to have it in June. He didn't have time to plan it. We had a church wedding, an informal one, but I wanted a formal wedding at the little Methodist church. But we didn't get to have it. Brother Dail said that we could still have our formal wedding when Doc came back, that he could take the marriage certificate and perform the ceremony. But he didn't come back.

Polly's second husband Gene Woodward . . .

Brother Dail married Gene and me. He baptized me. He buried all my family. I said he was always there for you when you needed him. Gene and I were going to get married at the Methodist church. But my daddy was in bad health and he wasn't able to go to the church, and I wanted him. It was my daddy's birthday, the second of October. So we got married at my daddy and mama's house. Brother Dail married us. Irma, my niece, was a little bitty girl about so big, and she remembers that she was up there. We kept her a lot. "Irma, you have to sit down on the couch," – we told her about it – "and you sit quiet and be quiet." And she did.

C.V. Williams was Gene's best man, and Velma stood up with me. I had a pale blue suit, one of those fancy ones that they had over at George's – you know S.H. George when they used to have their store over at Knoxville, their main store. Miller's and George's. They were real popular at that time. Ceconi. I had a pale blue. And I think a black velvet hat. We wore hats then, but now I hate them. And a corsage – I can't remember what kind of corsage I had. Gardenia, I believe.

Polly and Eugene Woodward, Polly's second husband.

I had known Gene for a long time. He ran around with my brothers, and we played ball. We played "Four-on-Deck" out there. And then we started going fishing together, and hiking together, and going to movies. We went to Harriman then. Oak Ridge wasn't there. We used to go every time the movie would change in Harriman.

Gene drove the school bus, and then he was working at the prison when he died, dropping those coal cars down. He hated it. That got on his nerves. He was sick, and he shouldn't have been doing that. A prisoner did it, but he always thought some morning that prisoner wasn't going to show up and he'd have to do it. He had a perfect horror of it. I was on a trip. He didn't want to go any place after he came home from the service. He said he'd seen all the world that he wanted to see. He was in the Philippines, and he was wounded there too. Shrapnel in the back of his head.

He and Paul Waldrop hunted and fished together all the time. They'd catch rabbits, and Paul would dress them and put them in the freezer. When they got a big mess, Gene would cook them when I was gone, because I wouldn't eat them. They'd always give some to my mother – she loved them too – cause he could fix the best. He was a good cook. He would cook the rabbits, and they'd have a rabbit feast.

Gene was graceful. For a big man, he was light on his feet. He was really a good dancer, and I liked to dance with him. A big man, you don't think of them as being so light, but he was.

I asked the doctor – he had been to the doctor the day before he killed himself – I went to see the doctor. I said, "Did you not know he was so depressed?" He said, "Indeed I did not. Had I known it, I would have sent him to another doctor. But," he said, "he would never tell you – you know that." And I said, "Yes, I know." When he'd go to the doctor, I'd say, "What did the doctor say about you?" "Well, he said he thought I'd live; he thought I'd make it a little while longer." He'd just give me a silly answer. But I never thought he would take his own life. He wanted me to go, and he would insist on me going places. We'd go out, he'd go with me. After church we'd go somewhere and eat. But then he'd rather just stay home and piddle around and work in his garden. He liked to make his garden. But I never thought he would . . .

I was gone to Niagra Falls in New York on a bus tour. They said that Sunday morning he was going to take my mother to church. My mother said he looked awful, he looked like death warmed over. Miss Hattie, she was the teacher, said his mind was somewhere else. She didn't believe he heard a word of what she said. Then he got in the car. He took my car and left his. I had a new car, and I had a gun. He took my gun. And he had a shirt – he sent his shirts to the laundry – a white shirt laid on the back seat when they found him.

When I came home, he wasn't here. He didn't show up that night. He never stayed out; he never went out at night. He didn't show up, and the next morning – I was up all night; I couldn't sleep wondering where he was – the next morning I was supposed to go to work, and my mother came up here and she said, "Polly, you might as well be prepared. There's something happened. Gene never stayed out all night." Velma and I went to Wartburg to the jail. Velma stayed in the car, and I went in. The sheriff was in there getting ready to go to court. He walked out of the bathroom with lather all over his face and his suspenders down and no shirt, and he said, "That man they're looking for, hunting for, is dead." Of course that just floored me. I went out and got Velma and she came in. The sheriff's wife was trying to find out – and me dying – but couldn't find out anything. Velma said, "Polly, let's go up to see Mr. Schubert *[Otto Schubert, the local funeral home director]*; he'll find out. Let's go." And we got in the car and went up there. Otto started calling, and he got all the information.

Said he was down at Soddy Daisy, on the way to Chattanooga. It was on a side road. Gene had never been there. I don't know how he found it. But it goes around and then comes back in Highway 27 up there. I've forgotten what they call that little community. It's just farmland is what it is. And he had gone across the railroad, in this wide place turned around and headed back. He wouldn't even know that road was there. And he was sitting there in the car playing the radio, and he'd smoked several cigarettes. A woman at six o'clock was going to work. She lived around there somewhere, and she saw it and she reported it and they found him. But he shot himself twice. I said, "I can't imagine."

We went down there and talked to the undertaker that got him. He came and sat in the car with me and talked to me. He said, "The reflexes – sometimes you pull the trigger the second time. The first one didn't kill him. The second one." Harvey Summers went down there and got my car and brought it back up and kept it at his house in the garage until we got rid of it and I got another car. I never saw the car anymore. I said I'd never forget Mr. Schubert for that. They were so good. Lots of times I'd think maybe he didn't do it; maybe somebody killed him. But he had money in his billfold. He was not robbed. I wondered about him having his shirt – why he had that shirt in there.

EMPLOYMENT

It seems that everyone in Petros – and, for that matter, Morgan County – knows Polly. One reason is that she worked for many years in the post office in Petros.

I worked in Knoxville for awhile after beauty school, but I didn't like it. So I came back home. I went to work in Loveman's Department Store in Oak Ridge. I just worked about three or four weeks, and Ellis Hobbs wanted me to come work at the post office for him in Petros. So I quit over there and went to work and worked 31 years at the post office before I retired.

My duties were everything, including sweeping the floor. They've got a new post office now; we had an old leaky one. We had to set out pans and catch the water when it rained. The roof leaked the whole time we were down there. I don't remember what I got. Not a lot. See, I didn't work full-time. I worked half-a-day Saturday by myself. Junior (George) Koontz, the postmaster, didn't work on Saturdays. I believe I got paid more by that, for working on Saturday half-a-day. But I worked Monday and Friday with him, and then on Saturday by myself. Only whenever I would work in the place of the postmaster, I got his salary. But for my clerk's salary, I just got paid for the hours I worked. Lots of times, if I just worked a half-a-day down here, Buster Kreis would call me to Lancing, and I'd go to Lancing and work the rest of the day out there.

I worked as the postmaster down here until they got a new one when they changed over. Then they wanted me to come to Oliver Springs. I said, "I can't see getting up at six o'clock on cold frosty mornings and driving over there," and I said I could retire by then. I said, "If you'd asked me a long time ago, I might have done it." But I just didn't do it. Then they asked me to come to Oak Ridge. They called me from Knoxville, and I said, "Do I have to go?" or "Are you going to make me go?" They said, "No. It's up to you, but you have to write a letter and refuse." So I did. I could have retired before I did, but Junior Koontz said, "Polly, stay, and we'll walk out together." And we did. We went out the same day. Junior Koontz. He was a good one.

What did she like about the job?

The people. Meeting the people. I never had a problem with anybody. They'd come from across the mountain over here, and we were not really supposed to write their money orders out. They were supposed to write their own money orders. But they'd come in and say, "Polly, would you fill that in for me? I forgot my glasses," or "I'm so nervous today I can't write," or some excuse. Well, rather than see them mess it up, I'd rather do it for them. And I couldn't say no anyway. We had one man he'd come in there and he'd drink that moonshine. Those little windows – he'd blow his breath through that window on me, and I'd be as drunk as he was. Always in the spring, they'd eat those ramps and come in there and blow their breath through there, and Junior would get sick. It made him sick. But I got drunk on that whiskey. He would nearly knock me down. And he'd say, "Polly, write me a money order to the Clinton *Utily* Board." So we had a lot of fun. But I never had a cross word. Junior and I never, Reece Liles and I never, Ellis Hobbs and I never – I worked for three different ones. I enjoyed every bit of it.

HOBBIES, CLUBS, ORGANIZATIONS

I've been going to the Home Demonstration Club *[now called Family and Consumer Education or "FCE"]* for a long time. I got a certificate for the first 25 years, but I've been going longer than that now. We used to have meetings in the church next to the prison. Susie Waldrop went, and Mrs. Donahue. Miss Lucy Alderson. I believe Blanche Armes went; she lived up there. Some of the women who lived up there went. Joann Solomon's mother. Pearl Harris. One time we had it down here where that old store building was, there across from the Baptist church where you go up to Bald Knob, before you cross the bridge on the left. Beecher Ward had a store there. Well, we had it there, and we had a hat contest. Everybody had one.

I'm an over 50-year member of the Eastern Star. I was one of the charter members. And I'm the only one, I guess, left. Ruth Jarnigan and Ray Schubert and I were the last ones. I don't go anymore because of the steps. Willie Bales said, "Polly, I miss you more than anybody at Eastern Star. When are you coming back?" I said, "When you get an elevator or something where I can get up and down the steps." She said, "You know, that's an idea. More of them could probably come." So they started working, and they've got a chair on the bannisters now that takes you up, and I've been twice.

Because I don't hear – I can't hear what they're saying – I don't know when to stand up and when to sit down or what. [Laughter] But I've been two or three times since they got the chair. The public installation, when they installed the officers this year, they wanted me to come, and I did. But I couldn't hear when they introduced me as being a 50-year-member. And, of course, I was supposed to stand up and take my bow, and I didn't. Ronnie Jackson came when I was fixing to leave, so he went with me cause it was open to the public. He said, "Polly, they're talking about you, that you're a 50-year-member." So I stood up. [Laughter] That's why I don't go; because I don't know what they're saying.

I go to the Senior Citizens meetings sometimes, and I'm a member of the genealogy group at Wartburg. I was a member of the C Club, but we've not kept that up.

TRAVEL ADVENTURES

I've been to Mexico about three times, and I've been to Canada I don't know how many times. Vera Beck and I took tours. When I'd get back, there'd be somewhere else to go. Vera and I went to Hawaii. We've been to the Bahamas about three times. We went to Florida all the time. *[Vera died shortly after this interview.]*

My cousin, Gladys Veal, took me to Florida every winter. I went down there when I'd lost my voice. She took me. She had two little girls. One of them had asthma, and she took her down there to spend the winter months. And I went. She'd call for me, and I'd go there. She'd get a house for the season. We had a maid. I didn't have to do anything. I'd take those kids to their dance classes, or we'd go to the beach and just have fun. I didn't have anything else to do.

Gladys got pregnant and had a little boy. She told her husband she was going to have the baby

Polly with a string of fish in Florida in 1954.

in March, and he was going to get off from work and go down and be there for the blessed event. Well, she had him on Valentine's Day. And it was just me and her. I was on a date. When I came in, she had her bag packed ready to go to the hospital. I went over there and before daylight that young-un was there, a little old boy. So I sent his father a telegram. I said, "Congratulations on your Valentine. It's a boy." And he called me back. He said, "What do you mean 'My Valentine'?" I said, "Exactly what I said. You've got a son." He couldn't believe it. She had told him it was going to be March. I will always believe that she didn't want him to be down there when that baby was born. So she and I had it by ourselves. And you know what? That baby – he told me he still had that telegram that I sent his daddy when he was born.

Well, I didn't tell you about my other friend who lived in Wartburg. She was an attorney. Mae Strickland. After my first husband died, she took me on my first plane ride. We went to Canada. She was a Grand Representative to Manitoba in the

Eastern Star. She was afraid that I would be air sick. She'd been on planes a lot, but I had never flown before. She got sick, and I didn't.

Then we'd go to Florida. She was into horse racing and dog racing. She loved to gamble. She couldn't drive. She would scare me to death. I'd hide my eyes. She'd straddle that line and cuss like a sailor. And cuss the other guy, but it was her fault. We went to Miami and stayed two months. I got tired of going, because I didn't bet; I didn't know anything about the horses. I liked to watch them run, but you get tired of that after a while. I wanted to go to the beach. We stayed with a widow that lived alone. She had a house and she rented out the rooms.

When Mae and I were getting ready to go to Florida, Betty, this cousin, popped in from Indiana. She and her husband had had a falling out, and she came to Mae's. Mae said, "Well, I'm not staying here with her, and I can't run her off. I'll just make her go with us." So she loaded her up and took her with us to Florida. I went to the

Polly being greeted by the captain of the cruise ship.

Polly on another cruise to the Bahamas.

races a few times, and then I got tired of it. My landlady and I – I said, "Let's go mail a letter," and we'd go mail a letter and I'd be too late to go to the horse races. They'd have to go without me. So Betty would go. Betty liked to go to the races. Mae said, "Polly, I don't believe you like to go to the races." I said, "Mae, I don't. In fact, I don't have the money to gamble, and I'm not interested in it. I like to see the horses run, but I've seen them now and I'd rather go to the beach." And she said, "Well, you and Margaret can go to the beach, and Betty will go with me to the races." So Margaret and I would go to the beach. Then Margaret had a boyfriend. Then I got one. He was Hungarian, I believe. He was American, but he was originally from Hungary. He's the one who brought me tea roses. We'd go to the beach and go places.

We were going to Cuba. That's when you could go get on the boat and go from Miami to Cuba. But Strickland decided she wanted to come back home. I believe she didn't want me to go to Cuba. This group was going to go. So I was mad at her cause I had to come home. She had some clients over in St. Petersburg. She still practiced law some. This old couple lived over there. They were rich and had a big house there and had one up in New Jersey. They went to New Jersey in the summer and stayed down there in the winter. So Strickland said, "I've got to go by St. Petersburg." So we went from Miami to St. Petersburg. The old couple fell in love with me. They wanted me to stay with them and chauffeur and drive. They couldn't drive. We'd go places, and we'd stay down there in the winter and go to New Jersey in the summer. They had a car as long as from here to there. I wouldn't do it. That made Strickland mad. I said, "You wouldn't let me stay in Miami and go to Cuba like I wanted to. I was on my way home, so I'm going to Petros." So I came home. She'd say, "Polly, they didn't have any children. They would have left you all their money. You could have been well-off." I said, "Who cares? I still want to go to Cuba." I never got to Cuba.

When I asked Polly where she would go if she could go anywhere in the world today, her answer came quickly.

I'd want to go to Switzerland. That's where the Bardills came from. I was working on my visa to go one time, but my friend Vera backed out. I didn't want to go by myself, and I didn't want to go with strangers. So I still want to go to Switzerland. They say it's beautiful. I've read a lot about it. The Bardills came from Switzerland, but the Goldbergs came from Germany. My daddy's side is English and Irish. They came from Ireland and England. So I'm a mixture.

TODAY

Polly and Bill Murray have been close friends for years. How did Polly and Bill meet?

I was working at the post office, and Bill and his mother lived in that big house as you turn towards Wartburg, past Raymond Jones' house. His mother got her mail at Petros. We were not allowed to tell them what they had when they'd call in, so rather than have her make a trip up there if she didn't have any mail, she'd say, "Have I got anything today?" and I said, "I don't believe I'd come today. I'd wait till tomorrow" if she didn't have anything worthwhile. Or, if she had something interesting, I said, "Well, I believe I'd come today and get my mail." Bill would be in the background, and he'd always tell her something to tell me. She'd say, "Bill said he still loves you." And I said, "Well, I still love him."

He was off on disability, and he said, "When I get my check started, I'm going to get me a new car, and then I will take you out to eat – you and Junior." *[Junior Koontz, the postmaster.]* So he got his check, and he went and bought him a new – I believe it was red – car. He said, "Look out there at my car." I looked out, and I said, "Whose is that?" He said, "It's mine. You want to go out to eat tonight?" He didn't ask Junior. I already had a date, but I said, "Well, I've got another appointment. I'll see if I can get out of it." It was somebody that, we didn't care, it wasn't serious. It wasn't a real sweetheart. So we went to Shoney's and ate. We ate shrimp. And it just started from that. That was the 12th of February, 1979.

For every occasion, he always gives me an orchid. I get a white one for Mother's Day, and I get one for Easter, for my birthday, and Christmas, and something else. I said I can figure out all these years and how many orchids he's given me. I don't need one when I die. I've already had mine.

Polly and her dear friend, Bill Murray.

Family reunions . . .

My mother only had one sister, and she was six years older than my mother. She had six boys and no girls. And my mother had four boys and two girls. So Velma and I were the sisters that they didn't have. Anytime they had a minute at all, they'd come from Indiana. They'd head for here. My cousin Arthur never missed a reunion, and I didn't either. We were the only two as long as we had it. Velma – we had it twice after she died. Then we quit having it. Arthur said, "Polly, did you ever think that you and I are the only two that's never missed a reunion of the Rogers?" And I said, "No, I hadn't thought about it." And he said, "Next year it may be just you."

Well, the next year I called. He always came down when the leaves turned; he loved to see the fall colors. That little tree out here at the Massengills' always turns first. I've got pictures of it and pictures of it. He has too. It started turning red in the top, and I called him. I said, "Arthur, you'd better get down here. Our tree's turning." But he said, "Well, Polly, I haven't felt good for a couple of days, but soon as I feel better I'll be down." I said, "You want me to come and get you?" He said, "No, I'll drive down." And the next day he went in the hospital and died with a heart attack. I couldn't take it any longer. So we just quit having them.

What's Polly's secret for her longevity? This is what she said:

Well, I've had a lot of health problems, especially in the last few years when my bones started breaking. I've broken both ankles, a wrist, my hip and six ribs. And now I've got this, I don't know what it is. Arthritis? I've never had an arthritis pain. It must have been though. It started right in that knee, and then it's gone up into my hip. That's the one that I broke. Maybe my screws are coming loose. But I just have a hard time walking. It's agony to put your foot down when I first get started. After I walk a little bit, it does better. But it sure does hurt. I hate to get up on it sometime. The doctor said, "You've got three screws in there." He's so funny. I said, "Well, when can I drive?" He said, "Well, now, the problem will be if you put the brake on sudden-like." I said, "I don't brake with that one. I brake with the left one." I had both ankles broken, and that one I had a cast on from my toes to here. I drove the car anyway. I braked with my left foot. And I can't go back; I still do it.

I go out to the funeral home, and they say, "Polly, did you come by yourself?" "Well, sure. You don't see anybody with me." "Did you drive?" They make me so mad saying that. I met some folks from Knoxville at the Red Lobster, and we were about half-way through eating and one of my cousins said, "Polly, how did you get here?" I said, "Well, I went out and started the car. I got in and started it. And here I am. Did you think I couldn't drive?"

They didn't see me when I had the cast on. I wore that cast – they put it on three different times. I had a bacteria in it. I went to four different bone doctors – none of them knew what to do with it. I had that cast on, my toes sticking out, and then I had crutches. Bill and I were going to meet Hugh, my brother, and his girlfriend in Tompkinsville, Kentucky, and go down on one of the lakes. We were going to spend the weekend. Bill lived out there across the road from Tommy Jones then. He came up here, and we loaded my car with food and drinks and fishing and camping stuff. But Bill got mad at me about something. I had had the cast put on the day before, and I didn't know if I could drive or not. He got mad at me, and he went home. He left me with all that food in the car and all that stuff, and I didn't know how to get hold of Hugh to tell him that we weren't coming. He was expecting us. So I said I will go if I have to crawl. I didn't know if I could drive or not, but I got in that car. But my foot would go to sleep after so long. That was the one that was on the gas, and it would go to sleep. I'd pull off and wake it up and go on. And, oh, Hugh liked to have died when he saw me. "Oh," he said, "I'd have been worried to death if I'd known you ..." But anyway we didn't go to the lake. We stayed there at her house and ate up the food and drinks.

The next day I came home. Bill could tell when I turned towards Petros. He knew every time I went by there if I didn't stop. So I went on like I was going to Oak Ridge and came up Miss Ruth's back road. That's the way I'd do when I was mad at him. I'd go down the back road so I wouldn't have to pass his house and he'd know I'd gone out. Minnie Hatfield and I were running around, and she never said anything for a long, long time, and I never told her. So one day, we were going down the back road, and she said, "You must be mad at Bill." And I said, "What makes you think that?" And she said, "I've just been noticing that whenever you're mad at him, you always . . ." I ran into Chiz Armes down there one time, and he told Bill about seeing me down there, so that ended that. He caught on.

But I don't know if he knows today that I went to Kentucky. I never told him. When I came back, then, I went on down and cut up the back way and came home and got me some more clothes. Called Hugh. He said, "You call me as soon as you get home. I'm going to worry about you." I called him, and I said, "I'm home." But I didn't tell him I was going somewhere else. I got me some more clothes, and I went to Gatlinburg. There was nothing; everything was full-up on Saturday. You couldn't get a reservation. So I came back to Knoxville. On Kingston Pike I found a motel with a swimming pool in it. I called Vera. I said, "Get yourself over here, and we'll spend the night. I've got us a motel, and you can go in swimming. I can't go swimming, but I can read." So I sat under the umbrella and read, and she stayed in the swimming pool. Then late Sunday evening, we came home.

We should all have the spirit and spunk that Polly has.

I've had a good life, but a bad one too. But I've survived it. It's funny. I have no regrets. I guess if I lived it over, I'd probably live it the same. I don't know if I'd change anything or not.

IMOGENE NELLE WHITUS EVANS

Imogene Nelle Whitus was born June 16, 1917. Her children call her "Jeannie." Some of her grandchildren and great-grandchildren call her "Granny Jeannie," and some call her "Mamaw." Over the years, hundreds of schoolchildren in Petros and Petros-Joyner called her "Miss Imogene" because she was our first, second or third grade teacher. I still call her "Miss Imogene." Ralph Waldo Emerson, American poet and philosopher, said that "to win the respect of intelligent people and the affection of children" is to have succeeded. Using that standard, Miss Imogene has certainly succeeded; she is one of the most beloved and respected people you could ever hope to meet. Here is some of her story, in her words and voice.

My daddy was William Gray Whitus. Daddy was born in 1891. His family came from Ireland in the 1600s to Virginia. West Virginia, too, I think. Daddy's father and mother lived in Murfreesboro, Tennessee.

Grandma Whitus' name was Nancy Lavinia Puckett Whitus. She was a tall, stately woman and had the prettiest hair. It was in little waves you wanted to touch. I believe Grandpa Whitus' name was George. He was a short man, and Grandma was real tall. There were five brothers: Uncle Walter, Uncle Bob, Uncle Charlie, Uncle Ed and my daddy, Gray. The sisters were Aunt Annie, Aunt Betty, Aunt Mary and Aunt Beulah. I think that was all. There was a big family of them so they all had to get out and work.

Imogene.

They had a big farm in Murfreesboro with all kinds of livestock and, I guess, a real nice house and everything. Grandpa Whitus got mad once and just up and moved. He left that farm and everything on it. They moved to Petros to what we call the "Hackworth House." Then they bought that little house nearby where Aunt Betty lived.

When Daddy's family moved from Rutherford County – Murfreesboro – their name was "Whitehurst." Over the years, it changed to "Whitus." That was in the 1890s to 1900. There's still a Whitehurst Bridge in Washington, DC.

They'd moved to Petros in the 1890s from Murfreesboro, and then Grandpa Whitus went back there. I think he came here to help build the prison at Oliver Springs, at Big Mountain. He worked there as a carpenter. They had to build a lot of things. The family didn't live here long till Grandpa died. They buried him in Murfreesboro. Grandmama stayed in Petros.

When my daddy was nine years old, his daddy died – that was in 1900 – and Daddy and Uncle Ed had to go to work in the mines even though they were just kids. I think Daddy completed the eighth grade, but he was self-taught and had a good education. He was an avid reader and was mechanically inclined. He had an equivalent-to-high-school education. But he had to go to work so young as there were four girls and five boys in the Whitus family to support.

Aunt Betty was next to the oldest. She worked in Nashville for years as a seamstress. She worked on men's clothes. She lost her sight in later years, and we thought maybe it was from working on those dark clothes and the lighting wasn't so good then.

A lot of people called my daddy "Prescott," and I didn't know why. I asked him one day. There was a Prescott's Store down there where Taylor's Store was in Petros, and Daddy helped them in there.

Miss Imogene's mother lived in Petros too, and that's where she met Gray Whitus.

My mother was Mary America Cooley Whitus. I don't know how she got her middle name. She didn't like it. She didn't like that at all, Mary America. She wouldn't tell anybody her name. I don't really know how she and my daddy met. She lived down at Ten Row across the railroad track up on a little hill where Logan Williams built a house. That's where Grandma Cooley lived. Most of Petros then was built surrounding the old powerhouse, near where Cotton Patrick lives today. That was how Petros was then. Up on the hill there, there was a lot of houses and that made up the main part of town. The Cooleys worked in the mines up on that hill. They worked there, and then they left town. Mama's oldest brother was Lum Cooley. He married and went to Alabama. He couldn't receive mail for "Lum Cooley" as there were a lot of Cooleys there, so he took Grandma's maiden name, Walls, and he went by Walls while there. She had two other brothers: Uncle Charlie, who lived in Kentucky, and Uncle Homer, who went to work in Detroit for the Ford Company. He worked there until he retired.

My grandmother's name was Edna Jane Walls Cooley. I never did know either one of my grandfathers. I never knew anything about my grandfather Cooley. I don't know his name, and I never saw a picture of him. Why is it you don't think of things like this until it's too late?

Miss Imogene's daddy always worked in the coal mines. When she was growing up, he was superintendent of the mines.

He was superintendent of the mines at the state. Brushy Mountain Prison was referred to as "the state." He worked there during the Depression. Of course the Depression hurt everybody, but it didn't hurt us too much because Daddy had a regular job and drew a regular salary. Daddy worked up at the state all his life. They just made about 50 cents a day in the mines when he first began, after his father's death. They'd go before daylight and get in after dark. They worked long and hard.

Imogene Whitus, 13 years old.

I was born in Petros. I think I was born in that little house of Mrs. Beene's, next to Aunt Betty's. There was a little house where Irene Bradley's mother, Granny Beene, lived. I know Mama said that I was so good and gained so much weight. I weighed 20 pounds when I was three months old. They called the doctor in, and he said, "I am surprised at you two women thinking something's wrong with a baby that sleeps all the time and gains weight like this, to not know that she's perfectly healthy."

I just had two brothers. I didn't have any sisters. I was the oldest, then Buddy was about 26 months younger, and then Pea. Between Buddy and Pea, there's 15 years difference. "Buddy" was a nickname. His name was Robert Gray. And nobody knows Pea's name. His name is Donald Evan. He was nicknamed "Sweet Pea" from the comics in the newspaper.

I was in high school when Mama was pregnant with Pea. I didn't know it. We didn't know things back then like we do now. Aunt Cora told me one night that Mama was pregnant. When Pea was born, Daddy got out on the front porch. He called everybody in to see his big boy – he weighed nearly 11 pounds – then he'd go out the back door, down the alley, and he'd call them in to see him. He was so proud of Pea.

That night, Mildred Hart and I and Miss Ruth Winton – she was teaching out at Wartburg – had been down to South Harriman to play ball and Miss Ruth brought us home. Pea was already born. I got to hold him, carry him through the house. Daddy was so excited. He said, "Get your things, Sis. I'm about to take you down to Hart's." But Mrs. Hart and Mildred were there. He was so excited about that boy. We all weighed 10 pounds or more. They say that's a sign, most of the time, that they'll have diabetes. Daddy told me there was some diabetes way back in the family, but none in ours.

We didn't run around like the kids do now. We stayed on that hill. We didn't go to town except if our mother sent us to the store. All the kids on the hill played – my family, the Slaughters, the Langleys, the Harts and the Joyners. Tom Evans' parents, Mary and Renfroe Evans, lived there with Mary's mother (Nellie Joyner) awhile. We played marbles, tag, hide-and-go-seek. George Jr. and Thomas Slaughter had a pogo stick, and we all played with it. Thomas had a little car, and we'd ride in it.

Imogene Whitus, George Buxton, Jr., Nellie Langley and Mildred Hart in 1934.

The Slaughters had a dog named "Spot," and we had a dog named "Spot." We called the dogs "Spot Slaughter" and "Spot Whitus." Every time the whistle blew at the prison – it would blow at seven in the morning, eleven-thirty and twelve noon, and then at four in the afternoon – those dogs would howl. Every time. Then they'd blow it if prisoners got out, to warn everybody. We didn't think anything about it because if prisoners got out, they were trying to get away from Petros.

I helped Mama all the time. I scrubbed the porches and did a few things like that for her. I took Home Ec, and on Sunday mornings Mama would want me to make biscuits for the family. I would. I loved doing it. Mama was such a good cook.

Mama died in 1949. She was so young when she died. Her doctor was from Clinton. He also worked across the mountain. They doctored her for nearly two years for asthma – and it was actually her heart the whole time. Daddy stayed over at Fort Sanders Hospital with Mama. She entered the hospital on December 17, 1948, and stayed until she died on January 4, 1949. Daddy had them do an autopsy on her, and the problem was a heart valve. And now that's just a commonplace thing to correct. Sometimes they don't even have to stay in the hospital to have that done now. My brother Don (Pea) is like one of my children. He lived with us since Mama died when he was 13.

Later, Miss Imogene's father married Della Stewart. Della had been widowed in 1941 when her husband, Dave Stewart, died after a coal mine accident.

Dell was a fine, Christian person. She was always helping somebody. Aunt Betty, who was blind, lived with Daddy and Dell. Later on, they moved to Clinton. My daddy always worked in all the elections. He was always interested in politics. After he moved to Clinton, he helped with elections there. You'd have thought the courthouse in Clinton was Daddy's. They were building it, and he thought it was the prettiest thing – and it is. It's beautiful. He enjoyed that so much.

LIFE IN PETROS

Petros was called "Joynersville" and "Richburg" before it became known as "Petros."

Petros was named three times. "Petros" is from the Greek word for "rock." I don't know who named it. I've never heard anybody say. Polly, Alice, Lucy and I are about the oldest people in Petros now, and if we don't know, I don't know who will. Of course, there were a lot of rocks there. Down from Lucy's house is that great big old rock. We've had pictures made down there a lot.

You know, Petros burned down three times. The first time was in 1905. I don't know where the fires started. *[In her book, PETROS: A JOURNEY BACK, Nellie Shipwash described a fire that threatened the town in 1928. At that time, the Standard Oil Company had a storage plant in Petros. The plant caught on fire and was destroyed. The town was in great danger of burning as well, but was saved. The storage plant was never rebuilt. Later, Lawrence and Mozell Duncan built and operated a grocery store on the site, and then the Gunter family operated their grocery store there.]*

It was incorporated a time or two. They had everything. At one time, Daddy worked down there at the bank. I guess he cleaned up and did everything. We had three trains coming in then. There was one in the morning, one at noon and one at night. One time, the men that came in were going to get on the train, and they accidentally locked Daddy up in the vault. They didn't know he was in there. But how was it? Just by accident somebody came and had to get in the bank and found him there.

Behind the old bank building and old restaurant – well, below Lucy Patrick's house there – is that slab of concrete. That was part of the bank. Then there was a doctor's office, Dr. Eblen. He worked across the mountain, then he'd come to Petros and doctor here. Then there was another building. It was a jewelry shop at one time, and then Mrs. Lehman had a bakery there. She would bake and deliver. Oh, she'd make the best bread! There was a pool hall in that next big building. Then I don't know what that was between that and the little library. You know it had been some kind of a building there. Aunt Beulah lived there at one time in the old pool room. Well, that's part of where that is now and also where Lou Adkisson Harris had that A-1 Restaurant. Next to Taylor's old store, there was a garage run by John Bennett. I think that place down there, between the old library and the old restaurant, was a garage too. But, anyhow, Bennett's house was there. We called it the old Portwood house. A teacher from Caryville lived in that house.

That was just a big cornfield where Baxter Trail lives now. Then there was the big Portwood house where Mr. and Mrs. M.L. Portwood lived. Their children were Arthur, Owen and Nina. That house was where Owen Portwood and Dorothy were married. I know when my family lived across the street, we would go over there and they'd sing. They could all sing – Owen and Arthur – and Nina could play. Dorothy could sing beautifully too. We'd go over there at night.

Owen, Arthur and Mr. Portwood ran a little store. When they'd go home for lunch, Nina and I would go down there and keep the store until they came back. Then we'd go home and eat. Mrs. Portwood was the best cook. Oh! She was such a cook. She was one of my idols. She was such a good Christian woman.

When Nina married Elbert Rogers and Irma was a little baby, I know she'd come up there and Nina – a beautiful and good Christian girl – had asthma and she couldn't breathe. She had it so bad. She'd sit in a straight chair. She'd put her hands down on the floor to breathe. And she had that little girl. Then Nina died, and Mrs. Portwood kept Irma then. She raised her till Elbert married Mary. Mrs. Portwood was such a lovely person. I'd go over there to Mama's with the kids, and Mrs. Portwood would sit there and talk awhile, and then she'd say, "Now, I'm going. You all have got family things to talk about. I'm going. I'll see you all." Oh, those were good times.

Petros had a ball team for years. Nobody could beat us. Down there where Ed Massengill lives, on that little hill there, you'd go down and there was the ballfield. Oh, Raymond Armes, Fane Smith – we had the best team. The Harts had a car and they took us everywhere they went. We'd go to Oneida and everywhere following them. Oh, they were good. I believe Mr. Kelly up at the prison managed the team. I guess it's just a vacant lot down there where the ballfield used to be.

We had everything. Up by Miss Lucy Alderson's was a lodge hall, White Hall. It was different. Down by Joan Haynes' house there was a big opera house. They had lodge meetings in that. They'd come here and put on shows, like *Robin Hood*. We had all kinds of shows. It was a beautiful opera house with a big stage. They'd also show movies. I know the DAR (Daughters of the American Revolution) – Mama belonged to that, I think. And then they had Red Men. That was a lodge too back then. I don't know anything about it. I don't remember if the Masons met there at one time or not.

I reckon we always had electricity. Growing up, I don't remember ever not having electricity. From that big power plant, they ran a line over to the Evans' house. That's when the family first got electricity there. The mines would close it down at twelve o'clock, and then turn it on the next day. Mrs. Quisenberry, who ran the drugstore, had a Delco. You could hear that thing running, putt, putt, putt. A Delco was power that you could get electric lights from. So Grandma Whitus got electricity from Mrs. Quisenberry. I guess that was the first electricity.

I've always heard of Fodderstack. That's where Black Diamond Coal Company was, up that way. There's a Fodderstack Mountain, I believe, isn't there? I'm not sure. Nellie and I went up there, but Nellie's husband said we didn't really find Fodderstack. But we went up there and thought we found it. It's Big Rock up there now, but it's changed since all that. You know where the bridge is, where you go up by Roger Duncan's, you cross that bridge? Well, it's on the right over there. Used to be a great big thing, but now it's changed. I guess worn down.

When my husband Bob was 15, I believe, a Sexton lived up at Petros – Freeman Sexton – and he had a mine back of the Evans' house. Bob was working in it, doing a few things in it, for the summer, and it fell in. Everybody ran out but Freeman. He came in there and got Bob. Bob nearly died. It fell on his chest, and it did something to his foot. He stayed home sick that year until he recovered.

Renfroe Evans, Bob's brother, was working at one time in Hazard, Kentucky. He was running a mine, and Bob went there and worked a little while. Then he came back and his daddy had a mine over there at Buffalo, a part of it, and Bob worked as a bookkeeper. He would walk across the mountain. Then he got a horse. He would come home every weekend but worked there during the week. His horse's name was "Bob." Well, one of the preachers at church that we had moved up on that mountain and Bob's mama let him borrow Bob's horse to ride up and down. But he got to plowing with Bob's horse, and it killed the horse. Bob loved that horse better than anything.

Several of the ladies told me there used to be a school at the state. This was a school for the children of prison employees. The school, discontinued in 1914, was also used for church and lodge meetings. I asked Miss Imogene if she knew where the school had stood. She told me it sat on the property, just down from the prison, that the state later used as a helicopter landing site.

Do you know where the helicopter landing is? That's where the state school was located. It is close to where Susie and Paul Waldrop lived. That used to be a state field, and then the house was built on that spot.

SCHOOLING

We lived up at the state while I was growing up. There was a house by the school in Petros, and Grandma lived in it. Mama wanted to move down so I could go to school. They brought me to the house where I live now – Nellie Langley's family lived there then – and introduced me to Nellie. Nellie said she just fell in love with me because I had blue eyes and black hair. They were all blond. And I thought she was the prettiest thing – and still do – I ever saw. I started school there. But they were ahead of me. I made a grade in one year and then I caught up with them. I was at the age that I couldn't attend that year. Miss Eva Summers, a teacher, boarded with Nellie's family, and Nellie went on to school. Mrs. Langley, Nellie's mother, was working in the post office at that time.

Fane Smith's mother was my first grade teacher, and Ruby Jackson from Coalfield was my second grade teacher. Fourth grade was Melba Carter. A Talley – I don't remember his name – was principal. Two of the teachers, Thelma Collins and Melba Carter, boarded out there at Joyner's. Where Lucy Patrick lives now was the Joyner house. Miss Eva Summers' brother, Laban Summers, would come sometimes and substitute.

Then they discontinued high school in Petros. High school kids had to go to Wartburg. Then we went to the school that burned. I believe we were in the seventh grade when we went to school there. Judson Taylor was the principal then. There were three houses lined up, near the school. They were nearly alike. We lived in the first one. Mrs. Slaughter lived in the second one. She boarded the preacher (Judson Taylor) and his wife for a year or two and then they moved to another house.

You know, teachers boarded with people then. I know Maggie Edmond kept Miss Eva Summers one year. Arnetta Quinn – Arnetta Beck – boarded with Mrs. Langley.

Did the teachers go to their own homes on weekends, or did they stay where they boarded the whole school year?

I think they stayed. I was just wondering one time about their washing. At Joyner's, she had a woman that stayed with her and helped her cook, and I guess she did the washing. There was a little house out there by Junior Wright's. There was a barn out there by Junior's, and there was a little house there, and she lived in that house. They called her "Aunt" something – I forget her name. I remember some Wilkes. They ran the store down there in the old Bedford building. They lived there. And then after them, I remember a Womack woman lived there. And then some more people. And then the Ashleys from the state. Mrs. Ashley was always a stately woman, and she always wore a lot of jewelry. She'd wear pearls down to her waist. She always dressed so nice.

SWEET MEMORIES

When Mama and Daddy married, there were two houses beside the Methodist church instead of one. Mama and Daddy got married, and they lived in that second house, the one that was torn down.

Oh, I could just go on and on about what I remember. Nellie, Mildred and I get together and maybe two of us remember something and the other one won't. When one cannot remember a lot of things, two of us can. Nellie lived where I live now, and I lived in the next house, and Mildred lived in the next one. We grew up there together. When we married and had children, we didn't see each other often but we were still close. Then we got to seeing each other more often after we retired. We all retired about the same time. *[Miss Imogene and Nellie are retired school teachers, and Mildred is a retired high school guidance counselor.]*

Imogene Whitus Evans, Mildred Hart Dillon and Nellie Langley Shipwash - friends since childhood - on the occasion of Mildred's retirement in May 1981.

I know one time Nellie's daddy had a car and it had a square back – I forget what kind it was – and we were ashamed of it. He took us to church out at Union, and we got down in the back seat so nobody would see us. If I'd been him, I would have put us out and I wouldn't have taken us.

Bill Schubert lived down there and had a garage where the Harts lived. It is where Mozell Duncan lives now. His son, Lawrence Schubert, had a car. I learned to drive on it. He helped me. It was a roadster, I think. It must have been a Chevrolet or Ford. That's mostly what they were then. My dad never did have a car. I don't know why. I was wondering about that not long ago, why Daddy never did get a car. They didn't think anything about walking miles to see anybody then.

When Miss Imogene and her friends got older, where did they go on dates?

Harriman was the place everybody went then because that was the nearest place. *["Oak Ridge" didn't exist yet.]* We went to Harriman to the Princess Theater. We went to ball games during the year. There wasn't much to do. We made our own fun.

Nellie, Mildred and I graduated from Wartburg Central High School in 1935. Mildred got married when she was in school. Nellie went to Lincoln Memorial University in Harrogate; she graduated from LMU. I think Mildred went there some, then she finished at the University of Tennessee. I attended UT and received a degree there. We've been friends all these years. Let's see – I was about five when

I met Nellie – it's 82 years that Nellie and I have been friends. And then Mildred moved up there when we were in the fourth grade, I think, when we were about nine. You don't find many friends as old as we are. But we enjoy life and each other.

I asked Miss Imogene if the three childhood friends still get together and celebrate their birthdays.

Yes. We don't always get together on the specific date, but we do have lunch occasionally. We went over to Nellie's for Mildred's birthday. Mildred was 87 in January, Nellie was 87 in April, and I was 87 in June.

MARRIAGE AND CHILDREN

Bob Evans' father and mother, Arthur Wiley and Emily Renfroe Evans, came to Petros from Roane County, Tennessee. Wiley was Superintendent and Engineer of the Brushy Mountain Coal Mines.

Bob's Grandmother and Granddaddy Renfroe moved in the house next to the cemetery across from the Methodist church. The Renfroes didn't have a stove, and Mama would cook biscuits for them in her stove each morning. I said, "Didn't think then that we'd be connected."

Bob came here from Harriman and lived with his grandparents. Bob was 17 years older than me, but it seemed as if I was older than him. [Laughter] I had known him all my life. He used to come to the house with Daddy. Well, I remember when I was four years old we lived up at

Robley ("Bob") Evans, Imogene's husband.

the state before we moved to town. Oh, it was sleeting snow. It was cold. And they came in. Bob had joined the Masonic Lodge that night. I remember Bob when I was four years old. And, no, I never would have thought growing up that I would marry him someday.

My family had moved back to the state. Bob and I got married while we were up there. We got married in Jamestown, Tennessee. We were just driving around one day, and he said, "Let's get married." We had planned to several times, but we just never had. We were married by a Methodist preacher at the parsonage. Seems like his name was Nelson, but I can't be sure. I wore a suit. A navy blue suit and a red blouse. We didn't have any guests because nobody knew it but Bob and me. That was October 25, 1936.

We lived there at the state with Mama and Daddy, and Bob worked there too. Our first child, Bobbie, was born there. Then, let's see, they changed governors. I believe it was Browning who was in. When they changed governors, they would change everybody up at the prison. You know when you work for the state how things happen if you don't vote for them. And you have to vote for the one you work for. Then if you lose out, you get fired. Daddy lost his job. Bob was working up there as an accountant. We wanted to keep the house so Mama and Daddy could live with us, and they said no. So we moved down in the administration building. It was located where the warden's house is now. It was state offices. Then they got big offices and they moved them all up to the new prison, and then people lived in the administration building. Bob and I lived upstairs. Mama and Daddy moved down there in that little house across from Portwood's Store. It belonged to Mrs. Jones, I think.

Miss Imogene and Bob have three daughters and one son.

Bobbie Jean is the oldest. Her birthday is August 7, 1937. Mary Emily's birthday is October 12, 1939. James Carr's birthday is August 17, 1944. (Jim was named after Dr. Carr.) And Sandra Ann's birthday is November 1, 1947. The only way I can remember the kids' ages, I remember Bobbie saying she's 20 years younger than me. And San is 30 years younger than me. Then Emily and Jim, I have to figure up their ages. I used to think that it was so silly when anybody couldn't remember their kids' ages. I said, "I see now."

Bobbie was born up at the house at the state. There was a house before you turn the road to go to Fork Mountain. It was on a curve, and there were more houses there too. She was born there on a Saturday morning. A doctor from the prison came down there. What was his name? I thought I wouldn't forget it. Seems like it was Metcalf or Mc-something. And Emily was born up at the administration building. We lived up there then, and Dr. Huff – he was a doctor up at the state, and he delivered her. And then Jim was born down there in the house of Dot's *[Bob's sister]* there where we lived.

Jim was premature. He was a seven-and-a-half-month baby, but his birth certificate states that he was nine months. But he was seven-and-a-half. His wrist wasn't as wide as Bob's thumb. I kept him in a toboggan – one of the kid's toboggans, he fit down in that – to keep him warm. Why, he didn't weigh four pounds I don't guess.

Bobbie's birthday was August 7, and Curtis Beene's was August the 7th, I believe, and I was going to have a party for both of them. A step was out on the back porch and there was a hole in the step and this dog of ours got out there and got her paw hung in it. I tried to set her paw free, and she bit me. That's one of the scars, and that's another one where I pried her mouth open. She bit me again up there. That evening she got out under the kids' playhouse and got to barking. I thought maybe she'd gone mad. I thought, "Well, it's nearly time for the baby to come." Dr. Carr prescribed bed rest for two weeks for me. Jim was born the night that I got up from bed rest.

I asked if she thought all the commotion with the dog made her go into premature labor.

Yes. I got to thinking the dog was mad and what it would do to the baby. Any time a dog is hurt, even if they're your own, don't do anything for them unless you have gloves on. When they're in pain, they will bite – not meaning to, you know, but hurting so bad. I got the dog's foot out, and then I had to pry her mouth open to get her loose from my arm. It scared her. So Lida Beene, Curtis' mother, had the birthday party for Bobbie and Curtis.

Sandra was born down there at the little house across from Portwood's Store. San reminds me of Mama a whole lot.

Miss Ruth would get after me. She said, "Why did you let them call you 'Jeannie' and 'Bob'?" Well, we lived with Mama and Daddy when Bobbie was born. Pea, my brother, was just two years old when Bobbie was born. So they said "Bob" and "Jeannie." Our kids just grew up with that. I didn't mind it, and Bob didn't mind it. But Miss Ruth didn't like them calling us that.

Today, with all the grandchildren and great-grandchildren, we've gotten so we can't fit into one house. For Christmas, we had brunch at the Doubletree in Oak Ridge. We had a good time.

Except for a short time in Crossville – and now when she lives in Knoxville with her daughter Sandra – Miss Imogene lived in Petros.

I've been right there on that hill by the Methodist church nearly all of my life. We moved to Crossville, Tennessee, when Bobbie was a baby. It was a time between the births of Bobbie and Emily. Bob worked there for awhile. But the mine was full of water and it didn't work out. I guess we lived there about a year.

Mr. E. L. Pardue, I think he was the Commissioner of Labor from Nashville, and Porter Dunlap – that was the finest gentleman I've ever met in my life. I've never met anybody any nicer than him. But they leased the mines at Isoline, about 10 miles out of Crossville. Mr. Pardue wanted to open a mine up, and he got Bob to go down there and try to. But it was just so far gone. Then they had a little store in there. He ran the store, and he worked in the mines too. We went down there when Bobbie was a baby. There was a girl that worked in the store. She helped me cook. I didn't know how to cook, and I had to wait on those men. They didn't stay there a long time. They'd come up on the weekends. We didn't have any furniture or anything, just the barest necessities. One time we had to carry the water from across the street. I was out there drawing water one Sunday night, and I looked and saw the kitchen on fire. I ran back, and we got the fire put out. I don't know what caused it. Seems like something on the stove caught fire. Then we moved back to Petros.

Later, another fire claimed the family's possessions. This one happened the week before Christmas in 1958.

Our house burned when we lived down at Aunt Betty's house. I guess it just needed rewiring. I had bought a new freezer. I had had it for some months, but I guess the wiring just couldn't carry all of it. I was in school, teaching. We were having chapel, and Gordon Wilson (the principal) came across the stage and said, "Imogene, come here a minute." He said, "I believe your house is on fire." Well, I went down there and, oh, it was gone. It was still there, but it was just ready to fall in. We had a little dog. Bobbie came and got her out. I had dry-cleaning laid out to take. And my rings, I had them there. I was going to have them cleaned. It was the 18th of December, and I had bought Christmas gifts and everything. We lost everything. Didn't save a thing. What you've lost, you don't realize. For years after, you'll think of something, "Where is that? What did I do with that?"

The house burned in 1958, and then we moved here and there. Bob went up and stayed with Dot, his sister. San and I went up and stayed with Emily and Robert. We lived there until January, and then we moved out to Liberty. Then we moved back to Petros, up on the Bungalow Hill above Ten Row. We just loved it there. There was so much history. Bob's uncle had lived up there – I can't think of his name right now – but they lived up there and they had big parties. They had power from the powerhouse down there. They had a porch all the way around it. Up there, you could see lights from everywhere. There were a lot of rooms. Lightning had struck up there numerous times, and the trees around had been struck by lightning too. But I loved it up there. I know one night it was snowing and San and I walked down and got Betty Patrick to come stay all night with us. We stopped at Mozell's store, and instead of just getting six drinks or something, I got a whole carton. We got sausage

Imogene and her husband, Bob Evans, in 1959.

and eggs, and I dropped the sausage in the snow. We all had a load going home, up that hill. Next day, we found the sausage in the snow. It was still okay.

From there we moved up to James Price's house, across from Emily. Then up to the Schoolhouse Hill. I think it was about 1961.

EMPLOYMENT

Daddy wanted me to go to Draughon's Business College, but Bob and I got married after I graduated from high school, and I had my family. I taught school one year before Jim was born. There was five years difference between Emily and Jim. That was back when they couldn't get enough teachers, back during the war. John Dillon was superintendent, and he hired me. My first salary was $52 a month. I had the first grade. And then I got pregnant with San. I taught two years, and then I didn't teach anymore until San started school.

When I first began teaching at Petros Elementary School, Miss Ruth Winton was the principal. From the beginning, I had lesson plans. They gave us a course of study. It had what I was supposed to do and accomplish. We had writing, reading, arithmetic, health and social studies. One year I taught the first, second and third grades together. I had about 40 students. It was something when you had three grades in one room. The third grade was my favorite grade to teach. They're so sweet. You just love them.

I was responsible for deciding if any of the children in my class should be held back. It was hard, but we had to keep the grades, and you went by that. Some children are talented in other ways besides learning. School was difficult for some of them. They should be in a vocational school instead of a regular school. In a vocational school they can learn to use their talent.

Parents would say, "Anything you want to do, you do it. If you want to paddle them, paddle them." We had their full cooperation in all of that. If we paddled them at school, then most of them got one at home too. I don't know if it's good that they're changing now or not. I guess it is.

At lunch time, each teacher had their own kids. We were with them the whole day. When my little boys would go to the bathroom, I'd go stand at the door because little boys like to wrestle around. We took week about on bus duty. You'd have to go to school before the first bus ran, and then stay there until the last bus ran of the evening. That was a hard week when you had bus duty. We did do it one day at a time, but that was so confusing we thought we'd take it a week at a time. You'd be tired by the time Friday came. There's a lot of responsibility and love being a teacher.

The old elementary school gym in Petros was so crowded. We didn't have any place for people to sit. We just had one bench all the way around the gym. The kids loved to go to the basketball games on Friday afternoons. I think kids had to pay to go, but it wasn't much. I don't know how we got them all in the gym, but I don't remember it being a problem.

I believe Petros-Joyner School opened in 1977. We went to different places looking at schools. We said what we wanted in the new school was a big auditorium and a gym. At Petros-Joyner, we didn't get either one. They had to rework the gym last year. We didn't have enough seats, but now they have these seats that fold up. They did fix a stage in the lunchroom. It's a beautiful school now.

The year they opened up Petros-Joyner Elementary School, I enjoyed that so much. John Jackson, the principal, would have devotional every morning for all the school. And I had it in my room too. It makes me so mad to see in the paper these atheists trying to do away with "under God" now in the Pledge of Allegiance.

We had a very active PTA, and they helped us. They would do anything for us. We had PTA meetings once a month. We also had carnivals. Sometimes we'd make a thousand dollars or more at the carnivals. We bought books or playground equipment or something the school needed.

Did she ever have a "bad day" teaching?

I guess I've had some, but I don't remember them now. I remember the good ones. If you were teaching something, you could just look at the kids' faces and see if they understood it. When they understood it, their little eyes would just shine. It really thrilled them.

One day I was having reading – I believe that was when I had three grades in my room – and Dr. Wilson (the Superintendent of Morgan County Schools) and several people with him came back to the reading group and sat down in little chairs. A little boy was reading, and he looked up at Dr. Wilson and said, "Can you read?" I remember that so well.

How do rural and urban schools compare?

There are pros and cons for each one. It's a lot different. City schools have a whole lot more to offer than we do in rural schools, but I think we have just as good students, and they perform as well as they do in city schools.

I went to school *[UT]* at night and in the summer. I would teach school – come in and do everything at home – go to school at night – then teach. It was hard. I don't know how I did it. Not all of the classes were in Knoxville; we would go to Oak Ridge for some classes. I graduated in 1974.

Miss Imogene was wearing a beautiful ring. She told me her husband gave it to her when she graduated from UT with a Bachelor of Science degree in education.

The UT ring has my birthstone for the setting. The year I graduated was the year that they decided you didn't have to come and walk through the line, so I didn't go walk through the line. I got my diploma later. Bob was sitting out at the playground – the kids were out playing – and he brought the UT diploma to me. It had come in the mail. It was hard; I don't know how I did it, to work and go to school. I think it's better for children to go on while they're young. It's easier for them to learn. After you get older, you have so many responsibilities.

Miss Imogene retired from teaching in 1980.

Bob had been sick about two years. He was bedfast, and San stayed with him while I was at school. Then I said, well, I'm going to retire. So I retired in 1980. Then he died in 1981.

Today, Miss Imogene's granddaughter, Jennifer Duncan Monroe, is following in her footsteps at Petros-Joyner. If she is anything like her grandmother, Miss Jennifer will have someone remembering her many, many years later as her favorite teacher – as I remember my third grade teacher, Miss Imogene.

MEMORIES OF PETROS UNITED METHODIST CHURCH

Petros United Methodist Church sits on the same hill where Miss Imogene and her friends Nellie and Mildred lived in the 1920s and 1930s. Miss Imogene's home today is directly across the road from the church. The official name of the road is "Schoolhouse Hill," although a schoolhouse hasn't been there for many years.

Mr. John Morelock from up at the state would bring his prisoners down there, and they built that church. Of course they would bring their dinner from the prison, but anything homemade, they loved. I know Mama, Mrs. Hart and other ladies would cook for them. The prisoners would have cornbread they brought, and they would fry it in a skillet. We loved it, and they'd let us have some. The church cost us $3,000. We got all that free labor, and I guess we just had to buy the lumber. The lumber now – oh, my goodness, what it would cost! Just one little plank is a fortune.

Before they built that church, the old one was torn down. It was kind of a gray color, I believe. You went in the door like we go in our door now, then there was a little lobby. The church sat north and south. It had a big basement under it; actually, it wasn't a basement, but a big room down there. They had a lot of lumber. We played there under the church. It was underground. We had church there by Lawrence and Mozell Duncan's house in a big building that used to be a store while the other church was being torn down and they were building the new one. The Bedfords had run the store there and lived in the part upstairs. Then that building became the Masonic Lodge and Eastern Star chapter for years and years until a new building was built.

The church building was a wine color, then green. It is still green today. The church is hoping to get the building painted in the near future. This church is such a blessing to my family and me.

Nellie Langley and Mildred Hart lived up there on the hill too. We lived in a row. Nellie and Mildred went to the Methodist church with me. Well, our eighth grade teacher, Judson Taylor, was a preacher down at the Baptist church. I went down there for their revival, and I professed and joined the Baptist church down there with them. That's a controversy Nellie, Mildred and I have. We were all baptized the same day. But Nellie said she was baptized up at Big Rock, and Mildred and I were baptized down there close to where there was a train track going up there and a bridge and a railroad track together. Nellie says she wasn't baptized with us. She was. The same day. Nellie says she's sure she was baptized up there. I said, "Well, maybe someday, Nellie, we'll know."

I stayed at the Baptist church for two years, then I came back to the Methodist. Mama and I went to church down there in the old building. Mama and I joined at the same time. They accepted my baptism down there, and I didn't have to be baptized or sprinkled again. I don't remember where Mama was baptized. It was in

1932 that we joined the Methodist church. And then it was after that, in the 1930s, that we got in the new church. It was one Easter.

Daddy said over there where I live now *[across the road from the church]* was just grown up with weeds and trees and things, and they cleared that off and they would have ice cream suppers and everything for the church. They had presiding elders then that were in charge of the church. They'd come every so often, and they'd stay down at Grandma Whitus'. She was one of the charter members there. I don't know when my daddy joined the Methodist church. It must have been way back.

One Christmas – I never will forget, and I've wanted one ever since – we went out and got a Christmas tree. It didn't have anything on it, just the limbs. We wrapped it in white crepe paper and put icicles all over every limb. That was the most beautiful tree. We had a big church then. All the rooms were numbered; all those rooms were filled with teachers, and we had young people. We have no young ones at all now. That's why our attendance has gone down.

Your Aunt Maudie Claiborne – every little kid went to her and loved her as their teacher. Everybody loved Maudie. She was the sweetest thing. She could sew beautifully. She was a good Christian woman. Her son Buster *[William Riley Claiborne]* died the night before my daughter Bobbie was born. He died down there in front of Emma Ruth White's. The truck, the peach truck, came in, and he was riding on the running board, and he fell off. It was so sad. Later, little Leon *[James Leon Claiborne, also Maudie's son]* was in my room at school. He was up there behind their house somewhere playing, and a log rolled over him. The third grade – we went down there when they had his funeral.

There used to be a parsonage next to the church, and we lived in it. From that first house on the corner, we moved to the parsonage. Then we'd get a preacher and we'd have to move back to this house. We moved over there twice and back. George Slaughter and Daddy made a radio. They worked out there on that radio in that empty house where we moved from, and it worked. They worked a long time. It was the time that Atwater-Kent came out with their radio. That's the first radio that I remember. They were advertising from Shreveport, Louisiana. That's where we got all the stations. I don't know if they named it, and I don't even know what they did with it.

We lived in the parsonage, then we had to move back over there to the other house when Brother Dail came. The Dails' daughter BeBe was born over there at the parsonage. I know they would spell words when we'd be over there. They'd think we couldn't spell, you know. They'd spell something about the baby they didn't want us to know, but we would know it.

I think we lived up at the state when we got our first television. I remember Dave Garroway on the *Today* program. I guess that was in 1954 or 1955, somewhere in there. My favorite program was *Lawrence Welk*. I still watch it on Saturday night. There was some preacher from Shreveport, Louisiana – I can't think of his name – but everybody liked him. We had a lot of good preachers then on radio and TV. Billy Graham is just wonderful and a powerful person. He is greatly believed and admired.

Miss Imogene, Alice Whitus, Polly Woodward, Hattie Simpson, Myrtle Delaney and Emma Rogers Lehman worshiped and quilted together.

We used to quilt in the back of the church. We'd leave a place and put our frames up there. Myrtle Delaney told us, "Now when I die, I want you all to be back here quilting and I'll be up front." We had the best time quilting. We quilted one for me up there one time. I got up and we looked, and I had quilted just on the top. I didn't know how to quilt then. I was glad it was mine. Then I went over that part and restitched. Oh, we'd quilt one or two a week. We made a lot of money, at three dollars. We'd have the top and everything, and we'd put it together and then we'd quilt it and sell it. We sold a lot. But three dollars then – you could buy a lot more for it than you can now.

Then we went up to Mrs. Lehman's to quilt. We quilted up there for several years. *At first Polly would cook because she didn't quilt.* But she learned to quilt and is the best quilter. But then Mrs. Lehman died, then Myrtle died after that, and then there was just Miss Hattie, Polly, Alice and me. We just disbanded. I love to quilt, but I haven't quilted in years.

When I asked her what her favorite songs are, Miss Imogene, with tears in her eyes, replied . . .

"He Lives." I like "Amazing Grace" too.

And her favorite Bible verse?

The one that we say at church for our little closing prayer. The 19th Psalm. "Let the words of my mouth, and the meditation of my heart, be acceptable in thy sight, O

Lord, my strength and my redeemer." Brother Dail, when he was here, he had us sing little choruses, Bible verses. That's one of them.

For as long as I can remember, Miss Imogene was the person who saw that the church house was heated, cooled, dusted, swept and kept organized. My memory wasn't too far off the mark; with the exception of a few years when her son or Bobby Whitus saw to it, Miss Imogene was indeed the person who readied the church for services, opened the doors, and then locked back up after everyone left. She also planted and took care of the flowers outside the church.

Jim, my son, was janitor over at the church for $15 a month. A lot of the time he wouldn't do it, and I'd do it. We had a coal furnace. A great big one. I think Mr. Riley Taylor gave it to the church. I had a wheelbarrow in the back room. We used one of the classrooms for the coal. I'd go over at two-thirty on Sunday morning, or three o'clock – winter, summer, anytime – and have that furnace fired up. It would get too hot – there was a pine wall there – and I'd sit over there a long time until it cooled down a little. Then we'd have to empty those ashes. Then we'd have to go upstairs and dust. With that coal stove, oh, when you'd open that door it just went everywhere. Then we went to oil. Then we had electric. Now we have gas, and that's the best and cleanest.

Before, when it would turn cold, I'd have to go over there and cut the water off so it wouldn't freeze. It would freeze every time it would snow and turn cold. I'd have to watch that. I kept a great big bucket of water over there if anybody had to use the bathroom so the commode could be flushed. When we used to have dinners – that old kitchen, the old cabinets – I'd have to go over there and wash all those dishes and things and clean up, fix the tables and carry food. That was a lot of trouble on weekends then. That was when I was still going to school. Lucy Patrick, Alice Whitus and our special friend Elizabeth Strange always helped clean up and arrange everything when the church had special days.

When I asked Miss Imogene how many years she took care of the church, her reply was characteristically humble.

Ever since I've been up on that hill. That was tithing. You know, if you tithe, the tenth you give is what you're supposed to do. But really what you're tithing – anything you do over, that is your tithing.

Miss Imogene did this until about two years ago. She lovingly credits her granddaughter Melanie Huckaby and Steve Davis with helping her the last 14 years. Melanie serves the Methodist church in many capacities, following in her grandmother's footsteps. Miss Imogene's daughter Emily has charge of the beautiful flowers now.

Petros United Methodist Church was blessed with talented musicians. One of them is Miss Imogene. For years she was church pianist.

I took music from Mrs. Laura Ford. She was a Joyner; she married a Ford. They had an office in the old administration building at the state. They had offices big as this room. She worked up there, and her husband worked there too. They lived in a big house. Mrs. Aileen Slaughter, I believe, taught music. Mildred took lessons, and Nellie took lessons too. We all played. Mildred played at the Baptist church for years. Nellie didn't play at church, but I have for years and years. I love to hear anybody play by ear; it is such a beautiful tone, and I love to listen to that.

My piano, I got it when I was four or five years old. I still have it. It was a player piano. A long time ago, we had painted the floor around the rug. We had a yellow cat – oh, it was the prettiest thing – and he liked to sleep up on the piano. On my piano, there's his footprint where he had leaped up there on it. And we didn't take it off.

Some of the pianists at our Methodist church included Mavis Carr, Aileen Slaughter, Polly Woodward and Lib Strange. I just thought the world of these ladies. Lib and I were great friends.

What's the origin of the organ at the back of the church?

I believe that Miss Hattie Simpson gave that to the church. It stays with the church. The organ up front is the one Polly Woodward gave us. I told Polly that we'd get together at the church and play sometime. We always played together.

I told Miss Imogene that she and Polly should get together and put on a concert. With a twinkle in her eye and a merry laugh, she replied, "We can't hear!"

Those big red song books at church – Roger Duncan gave us those in memory of Mrs. Lehman. I bought my grandson Jeff's piano and gave it to the church in memory of my husband Bob.

I remember the beautiful sound of church music when I was growing up – the chimes – that filled the air on Sunday mornings before it was time for the various churches in town to begin their Sunday morning services.

I believe when Aunt Cora Whitus died, the girls (her daughters) gave us the money to have those chimes put in. I played them all the time until someone said that it disturbed them on Sunday morning, so I quit playing them. Then I went back to playing them, and someone else complained. Well, then it got to where I couldn't get them fixed. After Irene Bradley died, her kids gave us some money to have them fixed, but I can't get anybody that knows how. I loved them. On Christmas Day, I'd play them all day long.

Well, the Petros Methodist Church has been there all my life. You know, when all you kids were growing up, I had no trouble planning Christmas programs because you all were there to participate. Then when you children grew up, we didn't have any more little ones to come in.

HOBBIES, INTERESTS AND ORGANIZATIONS

Miss Imogene told me that the four most important things in her life are her family, church, the Eastern Star and teaching.

I read all the time. I would not go in a house that didn't have books to read; I'd go crazy. When we lived down there at Dot's, we had the kids in the room with us, and we had a grate. I'd build up the fire and then I'd sit down there by that grate and read, cause I'd be so busy during the day that I didn't have time to read. I'd read by the fire light. I like so many authors. I get *Time* magazine, and I see where they've got a book about President Kennedy, a lot of unpublished pictures of him. I just thought he was the greatest thing ever was. I'm going to get it.

I support Cystic Fibrosis, Children's Hospital, St. Jude's Hospital. I think that I'd rather give it to children than to give it to older people now, because the young ones will be the older people coming on. I support them, and then a lot of my mail is wanting this and that, and I can't refuse. Cystic fibrosis is the next thing to what Brenda, my daughter-in-law, had. They're getting close to a cure, and I'll be so glad. And St. Jude's – they take patients; money is not considered. I got an appreciation diploma yesterday from St. Jude's. I help them too. I'd love to do something like that – have a hospital or something that helps children or older people.

I've been a member of Sunrise Chapter #364 of the Eastern Star for 58 years. I played piano at Eastern Star for 30 or more years. I quit two years ago. I got so tired I just had to rest. Nellie's daughter, Billie Lane, has been pianist for the last two years. Sunrise is a wonderful chapter.

Knowing Miss Imogene likes to travel, I asked her where she would go if she could go anywhere in the world.

I'd like to go to Jerusalem and just walk through there. I wouldn't go over there now. It would be scary. But I would like to walk where Jesus walked.

After Bob died in January 1981, Judy Caddell and John Owens came to me and said, "Let's go up to Gatlinburg and eat supper." We did. I started going places with Judy, John, Joan Haynes and Novella Jestes. We went on numerous trips and cruises. I went to Hawaii two times in a year, in 10 months. We went somewhere all the time. That's what helped me more than anything. I can't now. I can't go anywhere; I'm afraid I'll get sick or something. After I had one of my surgeries, I would get so sick. I could just be eating, and all at once just get sick and I'd have to lie down.

Imogene being greeted by the ship's captain on a cruise to the Bahamas in the mid-1980s.

My family and I went to my grandson Anthony's wedding in Miami Beach, and I tell you that was the prettiest thing I ever saw. Oh, it was beautiful. We went up on top of a hotel, and it was decorated with gold stars. Everything was beautiful. I said that was the best time we've ever had. Oh, everything was so nice. Anthony's wife Lara is a physical fitness expert/trainer. She goes with Jo Dee Messina, a country music singer, on her trips all the time, wherever she goes. Then when she's home, she works as a physical fitness trainer in Nashville.

TODAY

It tickles the kids to death when I send them an e-mail. I told them I couldn't hear. I lost my hearing aid. It didn't help me too much so I didn't buy another one. I just don't believe it would help – any of them – because the one I had was one of the best. And I know I pitched it in the garbage. I didn't mean to. They accused me of doing it on purpose. [Laughter] But I can't hear on the phone, hardly at all. So San does all the talking. Anthony, my grandson, said, "Well, good. We'll get to talk now via e-mail."

Miss Imogene is a breast cancer survivor. She had a mastectomy in 1995.

It didn't hurt me. I didn't know it. I found it. I went to Dr. Nelson at UT Hospital and got along fine. I don't have a bit of trouble. I had Shug Jestes praying for me. I believe she's a saint. She is, to me and to a lot of other people. It's been nine years now. I said I had that and didn't think anything about it. They said I could have had a lumpectomy, but I said at my age I'd just have the mastectomy. There were 13 lymph nodes they took out too. I broke my arm after that, in 1998, and I can't lift it up or anything. Can't write sometimes. I told Dr. Nelson at UT that I was having some hurting down there. He said, well, that was normal when you've had a mastectomy because of the nerves down my side. But I'd always thought it was from that broken arm. It's been weak ever since. My children said, "Jeannie, you didn't take therapy long enough." I said, "I'm not a therapy person."

Then I've had two or three more surgeries since. They've not bothered me either. I've outlived Daddy's and Mama's ages. My brother Pea used to tell me, "Jeannie, you've worked so hard you won't live to be 50." And here I've outlived Mama and Daddy and Bob. They all died at a younger age than me. I had been healthy up till I got in my late 70s. About five years ago, I had hyper-parathyroidism. Surgery was required; there's a scar on my neck. Then about two years ago, I had acid reflux and a bladder disease at the same time.

I don't know. I just always ate what was on my plate. We didn't think about eating then. I never did like sweet milk, but I can drink it. I had to take my medicine this morning, and I had to drink some. I can eat just about anything. I was a good cook when I was able to cook, but now I haven't made cornbread in about a year-and-a-half. I love cornbread. My favorite food is seafood; I love eating at Dandridge Seafood in Dandridge, Tennessee. Charlie and San take me there often.

I asked Miss Imogene if she ever had any bad habits, and I expected her answer to be "no." But she candidly told me that she used to smoke cigarettes. She didn't smoke much; she was sort of a "social smoker."

I smoked a long time. I quit close to 20 years ago.

When I asked Miss Imogene if she has a philosophy of life, she answered . . .

The Golden Rule. I would tell my children in school to memorize that and do that. That's my philosophy: "Do unto others as you would have others do unto you." I've told my kids that. I'm so proud of them. They're all so giving. They're not selfish. They want to help people. All of them do.

Miss Imogene is concerned for the future of the little church we all love so much.

I don't know what can be done. I asked Ed Nelson, a former pastor. I was worried, you know, they'll probably close it. I said, "Ed, I don't want that. But the conference didn't build that building. The Petros members had that building built, and that's ours. And I don't think they should take it." I believe Ed told me that they would take it, but they would someway give it back to us. But, now, I don't know what would happen. It worries me. I told Mel, my granddaughter, "Mel, I want you all to promise me that you all will stay there with that church so it won't go down." We don't have any new ones coming in or anything. My son Jim recently joined. That's more than we've had in I don't know when.

What does Miss Imogene think the world will be like in 25 years?

I can't imagine what it will be like. There's so many people in it now, and there's not room for the people that are here. I don't know about the religions – seems like some of them are taking over. I try to imagine sometimes, but the traffic, the people, the lives they live, transportation – that's going to be a problem. The Lord gave us this world. It was perfect, and look what we've done to it now. Smog, pollution, the population explosion, terrorism. I don't know; it's scary to think of it. I don't think it's going to last too much longer; I don't see how it can with the world the way it is now. It's never been this bad.

We couldn't make it without God, could we? What do people do who don't have God? I just wonder. I couldn't make it a day without Him.

In 1998, the church and town honored Miss Imogene with an "Appreciation Day." Sandra McDaniel and Emily Duncan shared the following information about this special day that was held for their mother:

The United Methodist Church of Petros, under the leadership of the Rev. Dr. Ed Nelson, set aside a day for the church and community to honor Mother on November 15, 1998.

The Day of Appreciation was a surprise event planned by Melanie Davis Huckaby, Steve Davis and Steve's brother, Rick Davis. Sandra kept Mother occupied until time for them to arrive. Melanie designed the program, beautifully decorated the sanctuary and the dining area, and planned the food and refreshments. Emily cleaned and "spiffed up" the sanctuary and dining area.

Mother's four children gave her a bouquet of roses. The children are: Bobbie and Eugene Duncan and family; Emily and Robert Duncan and family; Jim and Brenda Evans and family; Sandra and Charlie McDaniel and the Foster family. Mother's brother, Donald Whitus, and her stepsister, Lavena Cox, attended this special occasion.

Emily had the privilege of speaking, and she was delighted to have such a good mother to honor and to make mention of her mother's many talents in the church. Sandra also spoke about what a wonderful mother we have. Mother faithfully served as the church pianist for over 30 years. Her soft and gentle music is always a pleasure to hear. She "stoked the fires" from the old coal furnace to the oil furnace, and finally, the gas furnace, for many years. She would tend to the furnace late at night and early morning, making sure the church was warm, clean and in order. She prepared the linen and glassware for the Lord's Supper each time, and washed and cleaned all this after each communion. She planned the Christmas programs each year and erected and decorated the Christmas tree for the holidays. She was the "line of communication" for each pastor, advising them of inclement weather and other related matters. She was instrumental in all the reunions and festivities of the church, too numerous to mention, all of which were voluntary.

Jeff Foster spoke of his love for his grandmother. He told of the many acts of love and support she offered to each child and grandchild, and the words of encouragement she passed along to each one.

Nellie Shipwash and Mildred Dillon, two of the famous trio, were there to celebrate with Mother. Nellie spoke about how their lives are intertwined, and she talked about the controversial date for their baptisms. Mildred also spoke about their friendship throughout all the years. These three ladies, all retired teachers, have been friends since they were approximately five years old. Amazing!

Imogene surrounded by her family at an "Appreciation Day" held in her honor on November 15, 1998, at the Petros United Methodist Church. Family members are, front row: Jim Evans, Robert Duncan, Travis Duncan, Tory Duncan, Jackson Buckner and Tyler Duncan. Second row: Steven Davis, Casey Kennedy, Imogene Evans, Morgan Ford and Joseph Buckner. Third row: Duane Duncan, Melanie Huckaby, Cindy Scheve holding Parker Ford, Angie Buckner, Brenda Evans, Bobbie Duncan, Jennifer Monroe and Emily Duncan. Back row: Jeffrey Foster, Greg Duncan, Gil Hyde, Kim Hyde, Abbe Evans, Scotty Evans, Eugene Duncan, Charles McDaniel and Sandra McDaniel.

Judy Justice and Sandy Boshears sang "His Eye is on the Sparrow," while Doris West accompanied them on the piano. Doris attends early church at the Methodist and, at that time, played the piano when Mother was not feeling well. The program concluded with the congregation singing "He Lives," Mother's favorite hymn.

Our State Representative, John Mark Windle, and Morgan County Executive Tommy Kilby honored Mother with their presence and good wishes. John Mark remarked that he was pleased to be a part of the celebration for Mother, and he commented that the Methodist church is a beautiful structure. Tommy related his good thoughts about Mother and how she is consistently a good and civic-minded person.

All the attendees enjoyed a delicious buffet in the downstairs dining area. Gifts were not expected, but Mother received many beautiful items.

Miss Imogene is so deserving of all the best. Her family and all who know her recognize that she is truly one-of-a-kind.

ALICE LUCILLE BULLOCK WHITUS

FAMILY

I was born and raised in Arkansas. I grew up in Tulip, Arkansas. It lacked two votes one time becoming the capital. Tulip was just about like Petros. It had two churches and an elementary school and one or two stores. Other than that, we had to go out someplace to do big trading, then at Christmastime maybe to Malvern, Arkansas. I was born August 16, 1914. I'm two years older than Addie Mae, my sister. I was six years old when my brother Winfred was born.

I was a Bullock – and I hated that name worse than anything. It's an English name. My mama's name was Lillian. She was a Brumley before she married William Bullock, my papa. I started out saying "Daddy" like all children, but Mama said kids didn't say "Daddy" much then, and she made me start saying "Papa." I'll show you some pictures. Mama said some of them would get a camera and they'd go through the community making pictures. Well, Mama said there's a family there came by one day and

Alice.

she'd been washing. Mama had long hair at that time. Mama said that she told this woman, "Now I've been washing." And she said, "Just go in there and get in a dress. I'm going to make your-all's picture." Oh, Mama hated that picture worse than anything. Why, that looked pretty good. People slicked their hair back. Mama's hair was jet black. I had a good-looking father. Both of my parents were intelligent. My father was a farmer mostly.

William and Lillian (Brumley) Bullock with daughters Addie Mae (on Lillian's lap) and Alice Lucille, ca. 1917.

All of my people on my father's side came from Mississippi. My grandmother used to sit, and I'd listen to her tell about how they moved in a wagon from Mississippi. My grandparents had eight children, I believe, and they were all married. When they got too old, when they had to leave their home and were not able to take care of it, they'd just go and stay about two weeks with this one and that one and the other. That was the lifestyle of people back in those days if they owned a farm and got to where they couldn't feed the horses or farm and everything. There was no Social Security or anything.

I know in my mother's family – now I'm not just saying it – they were all smart. My great-grandfather on Mama's side came from Jerusalem. His whole family left Jerusalem and landed in South Carolina by boat. They were Jews. Their name was Simon. There were two sisters, but they didn't like it in the United States and they went back to Jerusalem. The men all stayed here. When the father died, they sent him back to Jerusalem to be buried. They say the Jews sprinkle gold dust in their eyes after they die, before they bury them. Now that's a Jewish tradition.

From South Carolina, they moved on further to the Smoky Mountains. They were farmers. I don't know what they did in Jerusalem. The children, part of them, were married here in the United States. My great-grandfather married an Irish girl. She was Irish and English. Fair and blond. Most of my great-grandpa's family – oh, their hair was black as it could be. Their daughter, Cornelia Simon, was my grandmother. I often wondered about how my grandparents settled in Arkansas, but Mama never did tell us that.

My grandpa on my mother's side, George Washington Brumley, was German and Dutch. A little short, pot-bellied man. He liked to talk. That's where this talking comes from. I don't do much anymore but talk. I guess I'll go out of this world talking. But I hope I'll be conscious enough to talk. I should have had an education to be a lecturer. I would like to have been a lecturer or a psychologist. I wish I could have had a college education, but I've got good common sense.

My mother was Cornelia Simon and George Washington Brumley's oldest child. Her name was Lillian Victoria. There was another name – Mama had three – but I can't think of it right now. She was named after one of the sisters of the father that came from Jerusalem; one of these aunts was Victoria. But, anyhow, being the first child – oh, I've heard Mama tell it. Said it came the worst snowstorm. In Arkansas it hardly ever comes a deep snow. That country, especially in the south, is just pine trees. And then they just had wagon roads from one house to the other. But Grandma took sick. It was about a mile or two to the Simons' farm. The Simons – now one of the boys was a postmaster and one of them was a doctor. So the night when Mama was born, Grandpa took a lantern and went and got Uncle Jack. I've forgotten all their names. But, oh, they said the pine trees were just laying across the road. They'd have to crawl over them and under them and everything. So when they went to name Mama, Grandpa told Grandma, said, "We're going to call her Lily White." They were going to name her Lillian, but he said, "Lily White." Grandma said, "I'm not going to have no 'White.'" He said, "Well, with that snow that I walked through to get that doctor to come here, you ought to call her 'Lily White.'" Mama said that was what he called her, "Lily White."

Alice and her mother, Lillian Bullock.

Mama had a wonderful mother. She had 12 children. Bigger kids, you know, would have to help with the housework and take care of the little kids. Grandma lost several children as infants. They didn't have prenatal care and things like that. Oh, Mama used to name the names of her little sisters and brothers and just sit and cry like everything. One of the daughters was 16 years old and had typhoid fever. People didn't have air-conditioning, and all people had big trees around the house. Oh, they lay with that – that typhoid fever – and this daughter, this 16-year-old girl, was recovering from typhoid fever. They had doctors, but they didn't have much medicine in those days. She had been sick so long. The doctor told them, "She's recovering, but don't let her eat any food that's kind of firm or hard in any way. You'll have to go easy with her and let her get where she can eat normal." Well, it was summertime and some of them brought in peaches. Everybody had an orchard. And she had been on just a little diet of nothing so long she wanted a peach. Grandpa peeled a peach and let her eat it, and that fever came back and she passed away in a day or two. We used to have her enlarged picture, and I'd lay on the bed sometimes and look at her and seemed like she was looking at me.

Then Grandma lost a son. We went down there to see him, and he was on a cot. He was sick quite awhile. He had told them, "Now I'm not going to be a farmer. I'm not staying on this farm." So he went off to a nearby town and went to work in a sawmill. I think he hitchhiked away. There were sawmills all over Arkansas. That was about the only job that a person could get. I can remember at three years old – I don't know how old you have to be for something to be said or done to remember it – but I remember us going to see him on that cot. He died at age 21.

And then it wasn't too long till Grandma died. Grandma couldn't stand anymore. I don't remember who brought the news. I remember somebody came. People didn't have phones, you know, and someone would ride up on a horse or mule. There were a few cars, not a lot of cars, then. Mama's people lived a good ways away; well, I'd say 25 miles or something. But I remember us getting in that wagon, going to that funeral, and she wanted the song "In the Sweet Bye and Bye." Certain things make an impression.

My daddy said when they lived there – they lived in the Simons' house – and Mama's mother would come spend the weekend with them maybe or something, he said he had seen her many moonlight nights at the cemetery just out from the garden and the house, out there sitting among her children. Now that's kind of sad. The doctor said, "There's nothing wrong with this lady's mind; she has had so much grief over the loss of her little babies, her little boys and girls. It's the grief she's gone through." Anyhow, Grandma died when she was about 56 years old.

The Jews had their own cemetery. Most cities have a Jewish cemetery, so there's some reason. Mama's family had their own cemetery. All Grandma's people were buried in the Simon Cemetery.

I remember Grandma. I remember us going and her picking the goose. Grandma was very talented. She was an organist, she taught organ. She was tall and she had very long hair. She could walk across the floor with a pan of water on her head and it never fell off. The best part – we went to visit and I sat in my daddy's lap and went to sleep. But I'd wake up every now and then and I'd hear Papa saying, "Well, Alice so-and-so." Of course being the oldest kid, you know, there I was pretending to be asleep, but I'd hear him call my name. Well, he was bragging on me or something.

Every one of Mama's sisters had coal black hair and brown eyes and the olive complexion. My sister Addie Mae had the big brown eyes, and I got the squinchy ones. Aunt Ella had a girl that had the prettiest black hair, and I just envied her. I was a little older. She married when she was about 16, but she married two or three times. They all ended, so I guess I was just about as well off; I just had one man. He wasn't the prettiest man in the world, but he was a hard-working man. I can say that. We got along about as well as anybody.

There was one brother didn't marry. Uncle John. Papa said he was high-tempered. Papa went down there to help farm one time, and he stayed about three months and he packed his clothes up. He and Mama – they were newly married – went back to where he was born and raised. Then there was a sister who was engaged to be married to a sailor and something happened. He went down on a ship or something. She never did marry. Uncle John took over the farm, with his cattle, and the sister lived there. Those houses were built with big halls through them. In Arkansas when they didn't have air-conditioning, you could sit in that hall – most people sat in the hall – and if there was a sign of a breeze, it came through that hall and kept people cool. It was wonderful sitting there. There were doors to the rooms if you wanted to go in. Well, this aunt had her bedroom on one side of the hall. She did the cooking, kept the house, kept the chickens. See, there wasn't any work for women then. He milked, I believe, the cows. He was so strict, but he told her, said, "All the money from the eggs and chickens is yours." So she would take off on Saturday evening and go to a little store if she had extra eggs and buy whatever she wanted, like soap and washing powder or just anything the little stores kept. Some of them kept dry goods.

When Mama was young, she would go and stay a couple of weeks with this uncle and aunt a lot of times. And this aunt dipped snuff. She was the one that got Mama dipping the snuff. They'd take the eggs and go to the store, and this aunt would buy her snuff. Uncle John caught up with her dipping, and he told her, said, "Now you can have all the money from the chickens and eggs, and I know you can buy your own snuff. I know you're dipping it." They'd wait till he got off out on the farm someplace, and Mama would be sitting there – Mama was about 10 or 12 years old – well, Mama wanted a dip. She'd let Mama take a little bit of it at first. It'll make you so sick. It made me so sick one time, I never did want another dip of snuff. I couldn't get up off that couch or hold my head up. It was on a Sunday morning – I never will forget it. They always kept a snuff bottle, a little brown bottle with a little neck on it, sitting above the fireplace.

SCHOOLING

There weren't many colleges. They had academies for girls, academies for higher education. Not many of them finished the 12th grade. But that was an educational place, I'll tell you. It was a farming country, but everybody believed in their kids going to school. People, farmers or not, they wanted their children to have an education, and they saw that they had enough clothes. They sold their cotton. Mama would go with my daddy on the last bale of cotton, and she would buy material to make us dresses. And they bought us shoes and a coat or something like that. We went to elementary school to the eighth grade, then we went to high school.

Estes Elementary School in Estes, Arkansas – that's where I started to school. I was nearly seven years old. Kids had to walk a long way. The school had two rooms. The elementary school was from the first to the fifth grade, and from the fifth then to the eighth. My first teacher, Mr. Louis Crowder, was a tall, slim man. He was married and had several children, but he lived in another community. None of us knew him when he came there, but I think he taught a couple of schools before I started. In this elementary school, he taught first grade up to the eighth. Well, there weren't too many students in each grade. Do you know he had some boys that were 17 or 18 years old? Those boys knew that this teacher wasn't a big and strong man. Any of those boys could have got ahold of him with one hand and thrown him down. They knew that they could whip him if they had to, that the teacher couldn't whip them. As a little child, we sat up near the front. The big boys and girls sat in the back. But do you know I can't remember him ever speaking a word to those boys? They'd pretend to be going up to the teacher with a book or something to ask a question, and they'd stop by their buddy's desk. They just had the little half desks. They would just stand on one leg and raise the other one up on the desk, and they'd stand there and talk as long as they wanted to. Mr. Crowder never said a word to them. Things have changed. I don't know whether they would get by with that.

I went to high school in Carthage, Arkansas. I finished May 28, 1933, from Carthage High School. I believe there were 12 that graduated. I was third in the class. It was a new school, just built. In the ninth grade, we had to go to the elementary school because they didn't have the schoolhouse completed. Then the next year we started, in the 10th grade.

The principal, Mr. Anders, was a little gray-headed man, not too tall. His wife taught English. I mean, she *knew* her English. She was a little gray-headed woman with long hair. Just a little ball in the back. They both went to college at the same place, but Mr. Anders thought he was smarter than anybody in the world. He made out like he preached a little bit one time. Boy, we'd see him coming up that little pathway – we could tell whether he was mad or not. Kids soon learn their teachers real good. Well, when things got kind of unruly among some of the grown boys or against something that he thought was not right in the school, he'd call a meeting – I don't know what you call it now, I can't think of it – and everybody would meet in the auditorium to listen to what was being said. He'd get up in there and, oh, he had a temper. He'd start out on whatever it was, and the longer he'd talk – it was his meeting – we'd get so bored we'd just want to cry – the louder he got. Oh, and he had a voice. All of us called him "Bull Anders." The boys would say, "We see Bull Anders coming, everybody!"

But Mrs. Anders was a sweet woman. Oh, she loved to talk too. And Shakespeare – she had taught it so long, she knew it by memory. She'd get up there and she didn't act it out, but she could read in such a way that it tickled us all to death. We didn't care. We'd just listen to her. We'd get by with a lot of things with her. I took Latin three years. Mrs. Anders taught it. A student could kind of choose what they wanted. I always had a desire to know some foreign language.

I've heard others talk about walking to school. Just like I did. I'd walk. It'd start raining or snowing. We lived about two miles. Me and my sister walked. It was a main highway. There weren't many cars, but it scared us to death because there was a low place and a bridge, and a lot of times there used to be a lot of – they call them "street people" now that stay on the street. These people would be without jobs or anything and they were maybe going someplace to hunt a job, and if night came they would sleep under the bridge. In dry weather there wasn't any water under there. Well, us kids knew that. We kind of came around a curve and the road kind of dipped down across that bridge, and then we had to go on up a quarter of a mile before there was a house anywhere. But we finally got a big black dog and that dog got to following us. That dog would bite if someone strange came around. Mama would always go out. And, oh, we would hate to have to walk – but rain, sleet or snow, that was part of going to school. But I felt happy. So that went on.

I asked Miss Whitus to tell me about her childhood friends.

Isla Samuels was one in elementary school, the first that I had, the main one. Natalie Smith was next, and Floy Vanlandingham. Another good, sweet girlfriend was Ruby Ross. She and I sat together in school. We were in the seventh grade. Her daddy had "John" to his name, but I don't think we called him "John." They had about eight or nine children. They were all married but the two youngest. Their mother named one "Ruby John" and the other girl "Ollie John." Well, they hated that. We were talking, and I called her "Ruby Fay." After that, she said, "Alice, call me 'Ruby Fay' because I don't like that 'Ruby John' that Mama put on my name. From now on, I am signing my name 'Ruby Fay.'" Oh, she was beautiful. Really all the boys were struck on her, and she knew she was pretty. She had real black hair, and they'd buy this stuff called – well, I'll swanny, it was on my tongue awhile ago – well, anyhow, it was white powder-like stuff. Seems like we'd mix it in a bottle. I went to using it because everybody just thought Ruby was so pretty. And she wore that black hair just kind of wavy-like. They called them "kiss-me curls." Did you ever hear of them? She could just bring it down here and then on the end just barely turn. But there was kind of a loop in it. You just kept it up over your eye there. Have you seen these Kewpie dolls?

In high school, Florence Wiley was a good friend. Her cousin was my first regular boyfriend. Seventeen years old before Mama ever let us date. His name was Ellis Wiley. At that time, the only place we got out in society was little country dances. Everybody had Victrolas. We danced with Victrolas. Well, there were a few musicians there, and once in awhile they'd play. My daddy never did like for us to go, but me and my sister, she was a good dancer, and it was just the community boys. We weren't struck on any of them or anything. We had a good time.

LIFE IN ARKANSAS

I have worked in the fields – all the young people used to work in the fields hoeing cotton and picking it – where these Union soldiers during the Civil War came in and burned this big two-story house. The people's name is "Smith" – that's an Old South name. We would see pieces of glass and, oh, it had burned and it just sticks together when it burns. We children would ask about it, and they said, "Why, the Union soldiers came through here and burned that house."

Corn was planted usually the first day of April or the first week. Cotton was planted I would say about the 18th or 20th of April. It began to warm up down south. That was cotton country, and you had to go out and beat grass out around the cotton so the cotton stalks would grow and mature. People would help each other get their cotton straightened out, get the grass out of it. I would go to the cotton patch – that's what we called all these fields – and hoe it. Up and down, up and down fields. Sometimes it would take two or three weeks to get a 20-acre field.

We picked cotton about August. That was the hottest time. I have picked cotton when it would be 100 degrees. The cotton matured then and, oh, it was thick. We'd put a strap on our shoulder and drag it up and down. Young kids would take one row, but most of the time two rows, and that cotton was high. The burrs stick in your hands. I've had them. But they mature, and those burrs burst open and there's the cotton. I picked 300 pounds one day. I wanted to. I wanted to see how much I could pick. No wonder my shoulders hurt so. But I was like my daddy. I loved farming. Freedom. There's freedom to have all of that.

The black people lived in a place called "Sixteen." The white people lived on the highway with all their farms. One farm right after another, with just a wire fence. But the black people lived in shacks on Section Sixteen. They had a school and a church.

Last night something came to me, and I got to thinking about Aunt Polly. Aunt Polly was an old black woman. A lot of old women used to be called "Aunt Polly." Aunt Polly had a well that didn't go dry, and a lot of white people had to carry water. I know a family – they were well-to-do, big landowners – and the old father of this bunch just rode his horse here and there and had the blacks working in the field. And this black woman had a daughter by this man. They were red-headed people. If you're going to pick up somebody, you'd better not pick up a red-headed anybody cause that's going to show up somewhere. But, anyhow, this girl when she was born and her hair started growing, it was red. I'd hear my parents talking sometimes. Not much passes kids' eyes and ears. Aunt Polly wasn't the only one that had children by the white men. That was very common in Arkansas.

There was another black woman called "Aunt Nellie." She was a little woman. Her husband built wells. Little bitty man. In the spring she had these yellow daffodils and all those flowers growing all around the fence in her yard. We went through the woods to her house, and her chickens – they didn't have much company and whenever they'd hear somebody coming up that trail, those roosters and chickens would start cackling and everything way before we got to the house. But we'd come through the back lot. All around the fence in her yard, she had those yellow daffodils. We girls, we were about 12 or 13, two or three of us would get together and we'd go through the woods on that trail. Aunt Nellie would always go out. It just thrilled her to death for us to come see her. We'd sit on the back porch, and she'd go out there and cut us big bouquets. For years and years we looked forward to going to Aunt Nellie's. After I left there, I'd always ask about them. They told me later that her husband was digging a well and it caved in on him and killed him.

I grew up with people that believed in long hair, especially my father's side of the family. When they started shingling the hair, we had a barber that came into the community and he would cut people's hair – children, grownups, anybody – for his training. That's the way he did it. Nobody paid him any money. Somebody might have dropped him a quarter once in a while. Some of our friends, Natalie and them, they always went out. They'd hear everything first seems like. So they came down to the house and they talked to Mama. They said, "Lillie, let us take Alice and Addie Mae over to this barber. He's cutting hair free. Let him cut their hair and give them a shingle." They all knew him. Well, Mama was for it. Mama was always for anything that was new. But, now, Papa was set in his ways. But they said, "We'll take them, and we'll bring them back." I think I was about 10 years old and Addie Mae was about eight. Well, we went over there. Natalie said, "You and I will never let Will," – they called my dad "Will" – "we'll never let Will know it. He won't pay that much attention." Well, we went, but all the time I was afraid of what my daddy might say. But we got the shingle bob – that's what they called it. I don't remember my daddy ever noticing it or ever saying anything about that.

When girls started wearing bobby socks, Papa said, "You girls are not going to wear bobby socks." Of course Natalie owned some. Papa said, "Now you girls are not wearing bobby socks." They thought it was sinful and everything, just like new things comes along now. We finally got us some bobby socks, and Papa, if he noticed them, he knew if it was all right with Mama he knew there wasn't no use saying anything, because she wasn't altogether boss, but she kept up with us, what we wore. Mama was the one who washed our clothes and took care of it.

In the winter that's when we started wearing thick, colored socks over the knee to school. A lot of us called them "rotten eggs." I believe it was "rattinag," but you know it sounds so much like "rotten egg" that we kids would say we had rotten egg stockings on. There were all colors, some black, but I didn't like black. I remember the first pair – a light orange color. It was a real thick stocking. It was a special knit too with a special kind of a design in it. Maybe one thread would be a little bit higher. They were neat and nice. They were warm. Oh, I remember Mama got me a pair for school. I think I was about in the fifth grade. It was cold winter and we had to have a fire. We'd pull our seats up around the stove and, oh, – because some of my friends, a little older, they were the girls that got them first and then we followed suit – I was so proud of those. I liked pretty colors when I was a little girl. You know how things are.

Boys would go off to get a job. There were big paper mills in southern Arkansas. That was the only jobs. But they'd get out of a job, some kind of layoff or something, and come back to their parents in Tulip, Arkansas. They'd come back home, and they'd meet up with girls and marry.

These boys had come back, and we were always in church. They'd walk us home from church. There's nothing like being walked from church. But, anyhow, we would walk, a group of us. My brother was a young man, and he would be in the crowd. It would be about 10 or 15 of us. Part of us would be couples. The boys, my brother and the others that didn't have someone to walk with, they'd walk ahead of us. Now a long time ago that's the way courting was done. If the father went to church on Sunday night, he carried that lantern and his daughters would have their dates walking. There wasn't much going to theaters, they were so far off and everything. Back a long time ago, when a boy and girl started courting, the boy would buy gum and give it to the girl.

I had one, well, he'd date me for awhile, then my sister. She'd always come in and take my boyfriends away. I can remember one Valentine's, he drove a school bus and he asked us sometimes – he asked me or my sister – on the last run to go and ride to deliver the last kid and then we'd ride back. He let us sit up on the seat by him. That was courting in our day.

I had a boyfriend that was electrocuted. He had just got a good job. He had another girlfriend. Just killed me cause I was afraid they were going to marry. He was older than all of us. That just killed us when we heard that this happened. It was a hot day, and he was sweaty. He was up, just ready to finish working on a tower, a high tower. But with the sweat on his body, he was fixing to come down, he touched a wrong – well, it's sad. I shouldn't tell this. I don't know why I'm telling this.

They didn't have mortuaries then. People "laid them out." That's what the saying was. I never did help. Addie Mae told me she helped before she married. She came home and said, "Me and someone washed that old lady and dressed her and everything for the funeral." I said, "Oh, Addie Mae, I don't believe I could have stood that."

Mama and her people, oh, they were politicians. I hardly knew what a Republican was until I came to East Tennessee. I know my daddy was called a "J.P." He wasn't a politician, but they made him one. My daddy was a farmer by trade. He did carpentry work between laying by the crops and harvest time. There were about two or three months in there that he would do carpentry work and sawmill work. He worked on the road during the Depression because a lot of times they were building new roads. Times were really hard. Nobody could really realize it. Papa was always a good worker. There wasn't a lazy bone in his body.

My parents left the farm after us kids all left home. They just stored the furniture and left everything and went to Malvern, Arkansas. It was about like Harriman. Papa was a night watchman. That's all he was able to do. Especially when they started getting old I'd leave down there and Papa would say, "One of these heart attacks will take me." We had to ride the bus from Camden, Arkansas, to Memphis, and I'd cry till I got to Memphis. My mother lived in Petros with me for 14 years after Papa died. My sister stayed here two or three years. We just had a wonderful time. We were so close.

Miss Whitus grew up in a Methodist church in Arkansas.

I was saved and joined the church when I was about 10 years old and my sister Addie Mae about eight. They had a revival. That's one thing that's wrong with the Methodist church – they've quit having revivals. Even the Baptist church. They used to have two revivals a year, one around Easter and Spring and one about October. But I remember we had a revival and people would fix supper or dinner for the preacher. Well, one of the preachers was an old man. Then they had a young preacher that was doing the preaching. The young man was a one-armed preacher. But both preachers went places. They didn't stomp their feet, but they got up and they really preached.

We never sat on the back seat of a church. Mama sat about the third seat. Mama and women with families carried an old quilt, but it would be clean. Well, I remember when she carried the blanket for us, the quilt. I guess Addie Mae was about two years old and I was about four. Little children get sleepy. That quilt was folded, put in between the seats, and people put their little sleeping children there. After the church service, we got in a wagon. We went to revivals in wagon days. The older people and the little children would sit in the wagons with whoever owned the wagon. That's about the way it was. And the young people did their courting walking behind the wagon. I can remember that as a child.

One summer we held our revival meetings out under the trees around the church because in Arkansas some of the days get 100 degrees. Now on Sunday we were in the church. But at this revival they had light. I guess it was coal oil in them, but they put them on the trees around, so it was light around. About 19 of us joined, professed Christ, and joined the church in that revival. I remember they sang this song, something about "Come home, come home." We sing it up here. It's an old Methodist song. But, you know, something would just touch me. I'd want to go up, but still I was small and everything and we didn't live close enough to go every Sunday to Sunday School. We looked forward to the revivals. But I remember the preacher – I don't know whether he talked to Mama and them and asked about us – but he just sat there and talked to me and Addie Mae. I'll bet her mind – she was always just a flittering – but we knew to behave ourselves in church. If we didn't, I guess Mama would have taken us out and whipped us real good. She'd tell us we had to be quiet.

Well, he began to talk to us about Christ and about salvation. I can't remember everything he said, but we listened. I remember I just listened real closely, and then he asked us did we believe in Christ, the questions that the preachers ask. We said, "Yes." Well, at the end of the revival – I think it went on about two weeks – he called on people to come up and confess their sins and profess Christ. I just can't remember all of it, but I knew what it was all about. It was the last night of the meeting, and I just stood there while they were singing for a long time. That song was "Softly and Tenderly." Well, something just kept saying, "Get up." I didn't know whether anyone else was going up besides me and Addie Mae, and I wasn't for sure about her, she was so young. But I finally – we were all standing while singing – just laid down my songbook and went up. Then they just began to come on up. One of the girls, I didn't know her at the time, she became one of my best friends and we talked so many times about it. But we were sprinkled. I believe immersion is the right way. The Bible teaches it. But being young and not knowing anything, I was sprinkled. There's some churches believe if you have not been immersed – but I have attended churches that accepted everybody.

We all had services in our community. Of course it was then Methodist, Baptist and Presbyterian. We'd leave the Methodist church – that was the biggest in Sunday School and church – and go on down to the Baptist church. But the Presbyterians just had a preacher once a month there. We'd just leave one church and go to the other, so I never did think of any distinction.

Mama fixed supper for the preachers. Our house had – all houses had – big wide halls, and the kitchen was always put way down at the dining room hall from the rest of the house. Well, I can remember after supper we were sitting in the hall out there and there was just a little breeze. It came through. There was no air conditioning. On Sunday, Mama and Daddy, the whole family, would argue the Bible. I said, "Law, if I ever grow up, I will not, regardless of what anybody believes or I believe, I will not argue on the Bible and what it says."

We lived in farming country. The little churches were a little further spaced than they are here in Petros. So where we lived and farmed, it was too far to walk every Sunday to the church. But we moved further down, closer in to the main part of this little town, and it was close enough for me to walk to church. That's when we started wearing high-heeled shoes. It was something to dress up and go to church on Sunday. Some people had cars, but out in the country they didn't. They had buggies. I can remember going to church in buggies many times pulled by the horses. My father read the Bible and everything. We'd be in bed sometimes and he'd read part of it to Mama. Sometimes I'd stop up my ears; if it was hell or something like that, I couldn't stand it. But, anyhow, I started going every Sunday. Walking. They put me to teaching the intermediate class there when I was about 16.

My mother joined the Methodist church when she was 14, but she was never happy in it. She and Papa's people, they were all Methodists. My daddy could quote scripture after scripture. When he went to Sunday School – and all his people were religious Methodists – they didn't have Sunday School material, books like we have, but they taught them from the Bible. And they taught them to memorize Bible verses. But do you know they have all gone Baptist? I went down to visit once, and my father told me – we were sitting in the swing – that he had joined the Baptist church there with Mama. They were right there close. All of the Bullocks as far back were Methodists. Well, one day Papa said, "Alice, if you don't join that Baptist church and be baptized, you won't ever get to heaven," or something. I thought – I didn't say anything – but I thought, "Papa, I never would have thought I'd have heard you say that."

EMPLOYMENT

After I got out of high school, oh, you couldn't get jobs anywhere then. But there was a paper mill. The men worked in the paper mill. Now, I worked in a factory where they made paper bags. They'd take this big thick round paper and make bags, huge, five-feet long, for sugar companies in Hawaii. They shipped them there, and they filled them with sugar and shipped them back to the United States. About a hundred pounds in a bag. But we girls made that. So I worked at that. It wasn't a regular job, but if they got extra orders then they'd call us in, and we could work at that. So that was the first money that I made. And I bought Addie Mae clothes. She was in her last year of high school. She loved pretty clothes. You could buy a nice crepe dress. You couldn't wash them. If they got wet, they'd pull up over your knees. But I bought me a blue crepe dress, and I bought her a green one.

I'm not bragging, but Addie Mae was just beautiful. Everybody would say, "Oh, she's the prettiest girl ever was." Well, she was. I'd get her perms and things. I don't have any regrets over my people. Even when I worked here at this library for $28 a month, I sent Mama a portion of my money. I have no regrets. I don't know how much money I gave my brother. They'd come here, stay, and get enough money to go back to Missouri. I was working. It was my money. Life hasn't been easy, but yet the Lord has blessed me.

I worked in Little Rock about three years during the war for Ford, Bacon & Davis, an ammunition factory. At the height of the war I worked seven days a week in this factory. I worked in St. Louis a little while, about two months. I didn't like Northern people. I said the North and South never did get along. I'd rather be a country girl. There's hard work and everything, but I enjoyed it.

Alice, on left, with coworkers at Ford, Bacon & Davis, an ammunition plant, in Little Rock, Arkansas.

"THE OAK RIDGE TALE"

We were all working in St. Louis. I went up there for my brother's wedding, and my sister lived up there. My brother Winfred – "Fred" they called him – heard about the Manhattan Project in Tennessee. He went over to Hot Springs, Arkansas, and signed up. They had a representative for hiring for war work in this building in Hot Springs. I never did know how my brother found out about it.

He came in one night, and he said, "Juanita *[his wife]*, I'm going to Tennessee to work. You want to go?" Of course, being young – they'd been married about two months – she said, "Yes, I'm going." I had gone to bed, and he said, "Alice, you want to go with us?" I said, "I don't know." They spent their money as fast as it came in, a young married couple, and I had always tried to save a little bit of money. Of course, they wanted me to go. I financed the way more or less.

Juanita and I went over the next day, and this guy was from Harriman. They had four men – from Washington State, Tennessee, and two other places. Well, my brother went with us and showed us. That guy from Harriman that was hiring, I'll never forget, he had – men used to wear gray sweaters, they were just kind of tight-fitting, they were cotton I think – but his whole elbow, his shirt was sticking out of that sweater. I guess it was so old it had just worn out. We hired in. I had worked for a company in Little Rock – Ford, Bacon & Davis – that made ammunition. That same company had a place over here in Oak Ridge. When I told him that, he said, "Well, would you like to work for this company?" I said, "Why, yes." He had a beautiful blond woman with him, and they took us to the station.

We – my brother, sister-in-law and I – all went to Oak Ridge together and stayed together. We got to Elza Gate, a four-inch snow on the ground, the 13th day of December, 1944. I won't ever forget that, with that four-inch snow on the ground. I guess there were 50 people there. They were getting hired in. We had another couple there from Arkansas with us. There's where they stopped us. They'd get all the information they needed and tell us where to go to work. Our first breakfast there was a place that made doughnuts.

They wanted us to go to the dormitory. The single people lived in dormitories. They said they were going to send me and Juanita to a dormitory. Well, I didn't want to stay by myself. So we just said, well, now somebody did promise us a trailer, and we said we were just going to hold out. They came up with us a trailer. They had one place where we took our showers. We wore shoes with soles, you know. And then they had places for us to wash. Usually we'd be six or eight people in there. That's the way. Most of those people were from around here or newly-married couples or something like that. It paid a little better wages per hour than it did in Little Rock, but the expenses were more.

They told us in Hot Springs, "Oh, they've got dry-cleaning shops, and this, that and the other. Just take a suitcase-full of clothes." Well, most of mine were wool skirts and things like that. A wool skirt had to be dry-cleaned. You'd stand one and two hours to get your dry-cleaning in and out, so I got to taking ours to Knoxville. I had to take it in and bring it back. Had to do all of it over there. I took my billfold and rode one of those cattle trucks to Knoxville. You walked up a flight of steps right there in town. When we first saw Gay Street, we thought, well, where's Main Street?

You couldn't buy anything hardly because everything had been put into the war. Aluminum and such as that. I would go to Knoxville, and the first things I bought were some little pots and pans. We had a little old white flame gas stove sitting up on kind of a little counter. We used white gas. Those stove eyes were open eyes, you know, with that gas. Good dishes would pop in two. I bought a few Pyrex dishes, but those Pyrex dishes would pop. We ate out all the time. We had all we wanted to eat, but we spent most of our time eating out because any place you passed was hotdogs or hamburgers or something. On weekends then we'd want vegetables, so we'd buy cabbage and just different things like that.

I went to church. There was a little non-denominational church. They called this the little, what was it? Chapel on the Hill? A lot of people got married there. Just a little church about like ours. On Sundays we didn't have to work. My brother and his wife didn't go to church, but being a young married couple I could kind of understand that. But, anyhow, I knew there was a little church up there. They had a different preacher each Sunday. There was one foot-stomping preacher. He was Baptist, and he was full of the spirit. That was all right. He had a family; they had left their home in North Carolina and come there. People were church-hungry because they had left their homes. I enjoyed going there, and I went there every Sunday. I liked Oak Ridge.

I worked at K-25 in the Leak Test Department. Of course, everything was very secret. Didn't nobody know we were ending the war. They said, "Don't even write home and mention anything about your job here. A lot of letters are opened to see what messages they're sending to people." They stressed secrecy so much.

We had a second shift. I didn't work Saturday or Sunday. Our machines were down across one of those long, huge buildings. Oh, the building was huge, wide as from here across to those houses over there. We tested pipe as long as this room or longer. The women had little machines, and the millwrights put the pipe on. It took two girls, one watching the meters on this little machine-of-a-thing. We covered it someway. We shot helium under that hood. I mean, if there's the least crack or anything, oh, those meters would just fly off. If there was helium in these machines, it would get caught. They'd have to send way down to the far end some place and – they called them "GI's" – they were Army engineers – they would come. Their clothes were a little uniform, kind of khaki-like. Some of the best-looking men you've ever seen.

There were about 12 or 15 of these machines two girls worked. So we would visit. We'd sit there an hour or more. I worked with a girl from Devonia. She would say "we-un-ses," and another word something like that. I thought, well, we never did say those kind of words in Arkansas; I wonder if that's English that people use here. She and I never had one cross word. She liked me.

My brother was an inspector. He was a good-looking guy, and he had so much pride. Many times he would borrow money to shine his shoes if he was going looking for a job. He went dressed up. Well, we'd just see him go through sometimes because his office was way down. Juanita, by having that operation *[an appendectomy]*, she worked at the desk in this big building where the man who was over all of us, Mr. Nutter, was. We had a lady from Virginia. She and her husband came to Oak Ridge to get work, and they had a trailer. She had three or four sons in the Army. She said, "Their shoes are sitting under the bed where they pulled them off to put on the uniform." Each one of them, she said, had their room, and she said, "I have left those clothes and shoes, everything in their room, like it was."

Well, Tommy Whitus was a boss on this. Every time I'd look across that room, Tommy Whitus was squatting down on some of those pipes or something, with a suit on. He carried his daddy's gold watch and fob. Tommy was born and raised in Petros. He would get cigarettes. The miners would get some lard and meat and a lot of cigarettes. Well, Tommy would get cigarettes, you know, and come in on the bus. He rode the bus. This girl from Devonia that I worked with rode too. We were all on the second shift. Well, he'd come up to the desk. He asked me to eat supper with him, go out about six o'clock in the evening.

My folks, my brother and sister-in-law, had gone back to Missouri. It was in July, I believe, when I moved from the trailer. I moved in a suitcase. I'm telling you, it was the stormiest weather one day. The lightning was striking everywhere. But I had to catch my bus to move into the dormitory. That was pretty good. The dormitories. The bus would take us up there. I had one of these women I worked with there in the Leak Test Department that helped me. She had been there long enough to know the place a little better. She took me to the school there and wanted to help me to get a school, but I had kind of made up my mind that I was tired of working in war plants.

I'll tell you like I told a guy in Oak Ridge. We rode the bus. I was on second shift, and people were sleepy and wanting to go to bed. They didn't talk too much on those buses. But this big fellow – it just happened that once in awhile we sat by each other. He didn't talk much, and I didn't either. But one night he asked me where I was from. I told him Arkansas. I never did lie about it. Someone in Petros told me many times she was in and out of Oak Ridge and she had to sign her name or something, and the clerk or some of them would say, "Well, where are you from?" She said, "I never would tell them I was from Petros. I would just say Morgan County." But this fellow said, "Oh, you're an Arkie." You know that will just boil in your blood. I didn't say anything for a few minutes. Then I said, "Let me tell you what I think about that. It's not where you're from, it's what you are." He said, "Yes, I'm from Arkansas too. I just thought I'd say that." And we got to talking then. He was friendly. He was holding two or three jobs in Oak Ridge. He was a professor at the University of Tennessee. But I didn't even meditate upon it. It just came in my mind to say that.

Well, after they dropped the bomb, Tommy left. One day I got a letter. The girl from Devonia brought me the letter, and in it Tommy said, "Well, I'm going back to the mines. I can make more money in the mines. John Lewis has got us all a union now and they have to pay us so much money and I'll make more. I'll keep in contact with you." Well, I just thought that's somebody I met, somebody that's gone. I wasn't deeply in love. There were men come and go, but I never dated one man. When we'd come in to work, we'd ride with different ones on a seat. One man asked me to get off and have coffee or something. But I told him, I don't know what I told him exactly, but I didn't want to get off. Most of them were married men away from their wives. I saw too many of them come in the back door.

They began to close those buildings. I and Lolita Goldberg, a girl from Wartburg – I didn't know where Wartburg was – and our woman boss from St. Louis were the last three women to walk out of that building. Some were placed here and there, and some went other places. They sent me then to that big Union Carbide building. I got lost every time I walked in there. Men rode bicycles from one end to the other. And we had a little room. You were supposed to have two years of chemistry to work there. Whatever was done there, we just had to watch big meters on the wall and everything and a man would ride up to the outside and unfasten something and take away something – I think it was a can or something. I saw them do it many times. I never did know what we were making or doing there. But by that time I was getting tired, and all my friends – some of them from Mississippi, North Carolina and everything – were moving or leaving.

Well, about the second letter, Tommy asked me what did I plan to do. If I was laid off over there, what was my plan? Was I going back to Arkansas, or back to St. Louis? Well, I got a letter from a boy I had met in St. Louis. He wrote me and asked me the same thing Tommy did. He wanted to know what I planned to do.

I lay on the bed one Sunday evening. I had kind of made up my mind that I was going. My mama and daddy were in St. Louis. Papa helped my sister's husband in the store, and Mama had come down with serious kidney trouble. I was making up my mind.

When I got the letter, Tommy, well, maybe he asked to come over. I would have to get a permit for him to come on inside. Oh, it was interesting. The bomb had been dropped, but the gates were still closed.

So Tommy came over one Sunday evening. I got him a pass. He asked me to marry him. He said, "Now I've got a little house in Petros." I didn't know where Petros was. He said, "I own it. My sister's living there now, but I told her I was going to get married."

I made a little more money when I came to Oak Ridge, but I had to pay the bills because my brother and his wife spent their money more or less for foolishness, I reckon. I never did see anything. So I didn't save anything. The only thing, I got a husband after I came here. I worked in Oak Ridge until September of 1945.

That's the Oak Ridge tale.

MARRIAGE AND CHILDREN

Tommy had asked me to marry him. I had a friend in St. Louis, and he wanted to know what I planned to do. But I didn't know. I lay there one day and it rained, and I'd try to think, "What am I going to tell either one of them?" I had never been to Oliver Springs, Petros and those places. It took me two or three days, but something just directed my mind to Tommy. But, anyhow, I think it must have been God's will. We didn't date very long.

We married the 4th of September, 1945. It was a Tuesday. We rode different buses that morning to Knoxville. A lady had told Tommy that you could get your blood test in the morning and go on to the courthouse and get your license and get married the same day, and that's what we did. I wore a blue suit with matching accessories. Some friends of the man who married us, who were there at the courthouse, served as our witnesses.

Tommy brought me right here, and I've been in this house ever since. I've never moved. Been here 59 years. If Tommy had stayed there – he left that job in Oak Ridge – I said I'd probably been living in a much better house than I'm living in. But he just said a coal miner is like a farmer. He just wanted to come back home again.

I said, "Now, Tommy, I'm not working anymore. I left the job. Now I expect you to take care of me until I find a job." Anyway, I've never had much. Tommy really didn't care.

Alice and her husband, Tommy Whitus.

Mrs. Whitus *[his mother]* said, "Now his daddy *[Ed]* was like that. Our family was just a-growing, the girls were growing up, and I told Ed one time, 'We have got to have a bigger house. Our family is getting too large for us all to be cooped up here in about three rooms.'" Every house then, people had beds even in the living room. You had to have it for the children. But, anyhow, Ed said, "Well, if you can get out and find one, I'll pay the rent on it and we'll rent our little house."

J.B., Tommy's brother, was in the Army when I came here. I remember he knocked at the door. I knew who it was because he had on a uniform. Tommy was in the back so I said, "Tommy's out there at the back." So he went on down. Well, after J.B left, Tommy came in and said J.B. had said, "Well, where did you meet that foreigner?" I said, "Foreigner?" He said, "Oh, that's just something to say about each other." Lots of boys were bringing wives from other places.

Now Tommy knew everyone because he was born and raised here. When I came here, they called me "Mrs. Whitus," and they called Tommy's mama "Cora" because she was raised here. It seemed funny at first being called "Mrs. Whitus." I'll tell you, he could tell me some tales – just like I'm telling tales. Nothing bad. All of Tommy's people, that generation's gone now. But that's the way – one generation passes and another comes on.

Francis and Suzanne Patrick were neighbors of Alice and Tommy.

I always called Mr. Patrick "Grandpa" Patrick because we carried water from over there. They were from Georgia. He had worked in the prisons there. Grandma Patrick – she was a nice woman. Tommy would go to work and then I'd take the buckets and go get water. Well, I'd always stop. She'd be sitting on the porch, talking. She told someone, "Oh, I feel so sorry for that little woman staying over there." Tommy left here to go across the mountain I guess as far back as they were mining. He left here at eight o'clock at night – someone picked him up – and he didn't get in till eight o'clock the next morning. And I didn't know one soul in Petros.

We were married two years before Thomas came along. I named Thomas after Tommy. His name was Thomas Richard. That Thomas Richard ran back three or four generations.

Petros, before I came and when the coal mines were around here, had a company doctor. Some of them lived right here, and I've heard their names called. They contracted with the State of Tennessee to treat the prisoners. But when I came here, the old doctors had retired except Dr. Carr. In those days when I first came here and started our family, women up until that time went to a midwife. But I told my husband, "Now, Tommy, I'm going to have prenatal checkups." He'd heard of it. He said, "Well, now, Irene Hobbs *[Tommy's cousin]* is a midwife, and she delivers most of the babies here in Petros." Well, now, Irene's civilized and had enough education that she knew it was important.

I had to ask around who were the good doctors and a person that could deliver a baby at the hospital. I went to Dr. Bowman at Harriman Hospital. I went to him for prenatal care. Our son Thomas was born February 28, 1947. I was by myself. That was the awfulest thing, having your first. My mother and sister weren't here. Mrs. Eva Peters, my neighbor, told me later, when I told her about the pains and everything, she said, "Alice, I knew they'd be coming but I wouldn't tell you –

because I had gone through it – because you were just so happy and pumped up, you know, and expecting your first baby."

Alice and Tommy with their new son, Thomas, in 1947.

I stayed in the hospital when Thomas was born for five days. My sister came and stayed with me a week. Did all the washing and everything. I didn't have an automatic washer then, but that's beside the point. I stayed in the bed, in all, nine days. Then I got up and just took over. There were no complications, and the baby was fine. Except he cried. I held him a couple of years. I always held my babies. I tried to go home to Arkansas once every year. It must have been about the next summer before my parents got to see my son.

HOME REMEDIES

One day Miss Whitus told me about a medicine women took if they were having trouble getting pregnant.

Women that couldn't conceive took Cardui. People just called it "Cardi" – you know how old people used to just call names. You'd see "Cardui" when you looked at the calendar. *[Calendars carried Cardui advertisements; in fact, you can still get calendars with Cardui ads on them.]* It was for women. Female diseases. It would bring on the periods in some. After they married, most of the time children came one after the other. There was no birth control at all. That's the reason there were so many children. I'll tell you another thing: in those 10- and 11-children families, usually there was always a child that was kind of deformed or something. I've often wondered whether it was having so many children or how come that, because I don't see that as much today.

One lady I know used Cardui, and she got pregnant right away. She had married real young. They were married I believe she said five years. She said they wanted children, but she didn't know why she didn't get pregnant. Well, that's when Cardui was on those calendars, and women began to talk. So she got a bottle of it. Seems like she said it took a bottle-and-a-half. She bought two bottles, I believe. But she said by the time that first bottle – she was pregnant then with her daughter. This Cardui was in a big bottle about a foot high. And it was black. They said that women took it one month, or took one bottle, then they could conceive and have a baby. But they took it for a lot of ailments. Well, Mama gave it to us for bellyaches and everything else. We kept a bottle. I couldn't read then, or I would have known what it was made out of. But I can't imagine.

My interest was piqued, so I looked up Cardui on the Museum of Menstruation and Women's Health Web site (www.mum.org). Here is Web site author Harry Finley's description of Cardui (reprinted with permission of Mr. Finley):

> *Cardui was a 38-proof patent medicine made from the late 19th century through the twentieth by the Chattanooga Medicine Company, of Chattanooga, Tennessee (U.S.A.).... Like most such medicine, I think it owed a lot of its powers to its high alcoholic content, 19% by volume, which is more than wine. And like most patent medicines, it promised to cure a huge range of ailments, many incurable even today. Cardui specifically claimed to relieve painful menstruation, which I'm sure it did, numbing the imbiber several days a month.*
>
> *In the 1960s, when I was at Johns Hopkins, I remember the pharmacist of a drugstore next to the campus telling me that elderly neighborhood ladies were the main purchasers of such medicine, its being an acceptable way to consume alcohol. Respectable women did not frequent liquor stores.*

The bottle label describes the contents as: "A Vegetable Bitter Tonic and Stomachic, with Antispasmodic Properties valuable in relieving Functional Dysmenorrhea (painful menstruation not due to alteration of organs)." The active ingredients are listed as Blessed Thistle, Black Haw and Golden Seal.

And Black Draught – "Black Draft" is what my grandpa called it – they took that for constipation. They'd take a pinch of it. Oh, it was strong. Both my grandfathers took it. Papa said that's what killed Mama's father. But it was a stroke. But, now, Grandpa Bullock took it too. It wouldn't be long till they'd go out behind the house. [Laughter] You don't know what we used to have. People didn't know what toilet paper was; they used catalog paper mostly if they were lucky enough to have a toilet, or they would use a cob instead of toilet paper. Would you believe that? Well, that was just kind of the men.

LIFE IN PETROS

Some people have asked, "What's the name of this place?" A history book I had told all about the beginning of it. The name of the book was *Tennessee History*. It was Tennessee history, dating back to about I'd say 1910 or something along there. It had been discarded. I think I sent this book to the principal at the school, and I never got it back. The way the history books tell it, they were marching along there and this man looked up and saw all those big rocks on the corner there that jag out. In Greek, rock is "petra." It's a Greek name. And this man said, "Let's call this place 'Petros' because that's a Greek word for rock. See all these rocks here?" So, the book said, they got with someone and that was where Petros got its name. That book was the only one that told about the naming of Petros. I've told several people that's asked, and some of them thought, well, that was correct. The Greek word for "rock" is called – it's not called "petros" – it's "petras." I've never seen the word "petros." People away from here, I go to Oak Ridge to the doctor, and they call me "Mrs. Whittus from Petras."

Tommy's mother's name was Cora. Dr. Koontz was her daddy. He came from Germany. He was educated there, and he came to Virginia as a young doctor. He married a Virginia girl, and then someway – I guess the coal mines – they drifted on in. For a long time they lived in Oliver Springs because that's where they were getting coal out of the mountains. They'd work them down so far, and the companies would move on.

Myrtle Delaney said when you called Dr. Koontz to the house if your child was sick, he'd come in and say, "Well, what's wrong with you? Stick out your tongue." I can remember when doctors – that was the first thing – "Stick out your tongue." And everybody said, "I believe you're bilious." Did you ever hear of that? *[Bilious refers to a sickly color caused by an excess of bile.]* Kids had diarrhea or were bilious. A child would take a high fever. Sometimes diarrhea. And kids in the winter had colds. Now that was the three diseases. And back then he'd say to a person, "Well, how's your bowels?"

Tommy's daddy was named Ed Whitus. The Whituses were from down in Middle Tennessee. Murfreesboro, Tennessee. There was a big bunch of boys in the Whitus family. They were called "Whitehurst" there. But from Murfreesboro they'd heard about the mines in East Tennessee so they left the farm – I don't know whether they sold it or not, I don't think they did – and they came here. Tommy's grandmother is buried in Petros, but the grandfather was buried in West Tennessee. He didn't like it here. But the mother stayed here because some of the boys were marrying. All the boys got jobs in the mines. Now they're all buried here.

Everybody had large families then, five and six. I think there were eight in Tommy's family. There were five girls: Inez, Lee, Louise, Marie and Emma Ruth. Their oldest child was a boy, and he died when he was about a year old. Tommy was the next boy. His younger brother was J.B.

They were the cleanest people. All of them were talented. His mother was a seamstress. She sewed for people to help bring in a little money. People said that the girls always had pretty little dresses because she could sew and she put ruffles and lace on them and everything. The father worked in the mines. Their father's grave was the first grave in the new Petros cemetery. There's a little plaque there by the Whitus tombstone that says first. These kids could go upstairs and see their daddy's grave over there. And they wouldn't stay another night, the girls wouldn't. The war was breaking out at that time, and the girls all went to work.

Tommy said that he went into the mines at the age of 16 with his daddy and worked, and he was never hurt. When I first came here, somebody got killed in the mines nearly every week. I got to reading about it. Up in Kentucky – that was all coal-mining country – I'd read in the paper one or two miners were killed. I tell you it got on my mind and worried me to death about him after he left Oak Ridge. But I never did say anything to him about leaving Oak Ridge. I felt like he knew what was best.

We'd go up to the schoolhouse for Mr. Slaughter's movies. Tommy thought he couldn't miss it. I didn't care that much about it, but I'd go with him. At the schoolhouse, once a week – I believe it was on Friday night – Mr. Slaughter had it set up. "Oh," Tommy would say, "let's have supper early and go." It would be full with people who worked at the prison. Adults. It would be full. He had a lot of funny things. Sometimes it was westerns. Good, clean movies. If there was popcorn,

I don't remember it, because there wasn't a popcorn machine up there. I don't remember how much he charged – not over 50 cents. But he made money by that, because that building was full of grown adults, a lot of people. I never did care much for a movie myself, but Tommy liked it. Then when we got TV, on Saturday nights the westerns would come on, and nobody saw anything until he saw his westerns, sometimes one or two.

I asked Miss Whitus what it was like being in Petros and having a newborn baby. Had she made friends by that time? Her answer makes me sad to look back at it for two reasons: first, because her friend Ruth died while we were working on this book, and second, because of the loneliness that I saw and heard in her answer.

Oh, yes. Many. Why, I wasn't here two days till Eva Peters and Ruth Jarnigan visited. Ruth, bless her heart, she and I have become closer friends here lately because she's one year older than I am. And both of us get lonesome. Neither one of us could drive or anything. I'd say, "Ruth, now, are you cooking or looking at something on TV or anything?" "Alice, I ain't doing nothing," she'd say. "Just call me. I'm going to get up after while and wash up my dishes." And I said, "Well, I always clean my kitchen before I go to bed." She told me many times, "I don't hook my storm door because I'm afraid the boys would have a hard time getting in if I died in the night or something." Well, that's good sense. But Ruth would come and visit. She'd sit over there.

MEMORIES OF PETROS METHODIST CHURCH

Tommy and I married in September 1945. I started attending the Methodist church in September 1945. The first Sunday I was here, they were having a memorial service at the Baptist church for Polly Woodward's first husband and two other men who were missing in action during the war. We had come into Petros on Saturday. We stayed at Tommy's mother's a couple of weeks because Emma Ruth, Tommy's sister, was living here in this house. We sat on the seat with Polly's mother and sister, Mrs. Rogers and Velma. I remember Velma had that big wide hat on. And Polly wasn't going anyplace because she was still so heartbroken. But Tommy had told me about this family – the Rogers family – working in the church up there, and the Whituses. They were all good friends. Well, we sat on the seat. They were the first two people that I met when I came here.

Then the next Sunday we went up to the Methodist church. I didn't know what church Tommy and his family belonged to or where they went to church. That wasn't discussed before we married. But during the week I found out that they all went up here to this church. Tommy told me he had joined the Baptist church. He said they had a preacher that came back, you know the preachers would go back and talk to the young people. He said, "If you don't join this church, if you die you'll go to hell." Tommy said, "He scared us into it. We said, 'Yeah, we'll join.'" I didn't know that for a long time. I thought he was Methodist.

It takes time to get acquainted. I just got acquainted with people by going up there, and then Tommy – we'd see somebody and he'd tell me who it was. So I've been going up there ever since. Here lately I've missed more than I have missed in a long time. After you get a little older, it's the difference. Our church now, there's about eight up here at the Methodist now that's pretty strong in their faith. We haven't let anything faze us yet. Our families up there were just kind of like one big family. We all just love each other's children and everything.

Our church belongs to the Holston Conference. Now the question came up about if this church door closes, there weren't enough people to carry on, what was going to be done with the church furniture and the land, if we had any money or anything. Imogene said she asked her children, "Don't ever let the doors of this church close." There's just about seven or eight that go to church every Sunday now. It's gone to that.

Those chairs up front belong to this Methodist church. When I came here, the leather bottoms had worn out. The straw and the springs were sticking up in some of them. We organized what we called "Ladies Aide" at first. The Methodist church, after it consolidated, the Women's Society was called "WSCS" – that was "Women's Society of Christian Service." We paid dues, 25 cents a month, and there were just about six of us women that attended every week. But we carried out the instructions from the United Methodist Church on how to conduct our meetings, and we studied missionaries and such as that. We took that money, and Mrs. Lehman had a friend that used to come to this church that married a man in Clinton and he had an upholstery shop. We raised enough money with these little dues and everything that she sent these chairs over there and he reupholstered them, put new leather in the seat of them, fixed the springs, and put on another light varnish. They're beautiful chairs. They belong to the Methodist church. When we talked about the doors closing, what would happen, Imogene was awfully worried about it. I wasn't worried, but at the same time there was a Methodist church in Knoxville that didn't have enough members to hold on.

When I started going to the Methodist church in 1945, I would say an average of 60 people went. The first preacher – I told Lucy the other night when we were talking about it – I said the first preacher was a foot-stomping preacher. She said, "Why, Alice, I don't remember that." The Methodist church – I can never remember a preacher stomping the floor, but this fellow would. She began to name them over, and she came to a "Bray." Lucy said, "Was it 'Bray'?" I said, "Bray was right."

We had a little trail; we'd walk up that trail to the church. We used to have a parsonage. The preachers all lived there. Preacher Allison was one that everybody liked. He had been here before I came. He would just come through here visiting, walking – I don't know where he'd park his car. He went and visited with Mrs. Barger, my neighbor. They were all Baptists. He didn't care whether they were Baptist or anything.

The Holston Conference Church, since I've been here, preached at three churches. It's Petros, Jonesville and Oliver Springs now. I have had history books at the library that gave the history of the first circuit riders. They were paid in potatoes, vegetables. The doctors also. I told Ralph Carr one day, I said, "Well, Ralph, you were the only child in your family. Your father was a doctor. I guess you could do or have more than others." He said, "Alice, my daddy was a doctor, but he never did get much money. People – he'd go to their homes just like the preachers would visit in homes – somebody would give him a bushel of Irish potatoes. Somebody would give him a couple dozen eggs. He actually got more pay like that because at that time most everybody here in Petros that's the way they paid him." And they paid the preachers. They all had a good horse and they rode. But that was part of history. In Arkansas it was the same way.

I wasn't here I don't believe a year when they put me as Sunday School teacher of the kindergarten class downstairs. The only one I remember real well was Emily Evans. She'd sit there in one of those little chairs, never open her mouth. I guess there were 10 or 12 children. Then I had, as the children grew up, the intermediates. That was Judy and Jerry Duncan, Pat and Bill Patrick, my son Thomas, and the Waldrop girls. We had so many members coming. That's when we had the largest number of members.

Brother Dail was here, and I remember the Sunday he came down and I was teaching the intermediates. He said, "Alice, do you mind to stop the class? I want to talk to your Sunday School group." I didn't know what he was going to talk about. I said, "Yes. We're about through with the lesson. You just go ahead." So we were all sitting down there, and he started. He talked to the whole class about being a Christian, about accepting Christ. Well, it was more or less the salvation story in a short form. And every one of them kids told him yes when he asked them did they want to become Christians, did they want to join the church.

Alice.

That was the last large group I had, but I taught that class as long as we had children. Gail Patrick and my son Bobby were the last two that I taught. We talked it over. I said, "Well," – they were up in their teens – "there's just no use of coming down here for just the two of you. If we had visitors sometimes Sunday it would be different, but you all are old enough to understand the adult Sunday School lesson." So they came on upstairs. Hattie Simpson taught the adult class, and then I believe Elizabeth Strange took Miss Hattie's place. She taught the class until Mr. Strange retired and they left here. Then I began teaching the adult class.

We had a Wednesday night service. Mrs. Strange had a little old car, and she would pick up Mrs. Moore, the warden's wife. She'd stop here and pick me up. We'd go on up and pick up Myrtle Delaney. That's all I remember. We were just stuffed in the car, but it wasn't a long drive.

Myrtle Delaney grew up in that church and, oh, she loved her church. I hope you put something about Myrtle Delaney in this book. If there was going to be a dinner or something on Sunday, at her age, when she was 80 years old, she ran up and down that hill to the church to see if everything was just so-so and clean.

Each summer the church always had a Vacation Bible School. I helped with Bible School because I had worked on it at home. I think it did have a great meaning on the younger people and they all enjoyed it.

I've been a lay leader in our church for a long time. I've been a speaker on a lot of things, but not lately.

I asked Miss Whitus what her favorite Bible verse is and what her favorite song is.

I had to look it up for Myrtle Delaney because she wanted it read in her burial service. "I have fought the good fight. I have finished my course, and I am now ready to be offered up." It's in 2 Timothy. *["I have fought the good fight, I have finished the race, I have kept the faith. Now there is in store for me the crown of righteousness, which the Lord, the righteous Judge, will award to me on that day – and not only to me, but also to all who have longed for his appearing." 2 Timothy 4:7-8 NIV]* Myrtle came to the library one day and asked me where that could be found. She said, "I've looked and looked and couldn't find it."

My favorite song? "Beautiful Star of Bethlehem" – that's it.

I asked Miss Whitus what she thinks the world will be like in 25 years.

I don't believe the world will be standing. No one but God the Father knows. Mr. and Mrs. Joe Peters got me to listening to Charles Stanley. Mrs. Peters said, "Oh, Alice, he's the greatest preacher. I said, 'Kathryn *[Mrs. Peters' daughter]*, don't you all call me at a certain time that he's on. I take my phone off the hook because I don't want anybody calling and bothering me when Charles Stanley is on.'" I then got to listening to him, and when Addie Mae was here, she liked to listen to him. Charles Stanley said that he preached the end of time so much when he first went to Atlanta, Georgia, that he thought the congregation got tired of hearing it. But, they're not preaching that so much now. I just hardly ever hear any of them preach it. But several years ago, they were just preaching it going and coming. A lot of them said Jesus may come, or Jesus will come, in 1981. Well, Jesus didn't come then.

Our little church, it hasn't always been perfect; none of the churches are perfect. But it will be perfect when Jesus comes, cause he's coming to take the Christians away. But, from reading the scripture and then hearing others, God gave Jesus power, put everything under his feet, that meant power, except the time for Jesus' return for his church. There's people that say, "Well, it could be anytime."

I read the devotional called *Bread of Life*, and then our church still gets *The Upper Room*. I do my Bible reading after I go to bed at night. Seems like it's just comforting to read. Some days it will just hit you. Oh, the promises of God that he will never leave us. That's just good for me to lay down there by myself. He gives me comfort in going to sleep.

Jesus was born as a baby, but he was God. Now, that's a mystery and I don't understand it. I've heard preachers say there are many mysteries that we will never know until we get to heaven.

I asked what she thinks heaven is like.

In the Book of Revelation they use symbols and things to illustrate what heaven's going to be. Streets of gold. But, oh, it used to, when I was little and my daddy would be reading it, it scared me half to death. A lot of people say, "I can't read Revelation."

Here, Miss Whitus spoke to me of my 14-year-old daughter Casey who died in 1996.

I think the Bible says there's times to give sympathy. Now you – I'm bringing up something that might hurt you – you will never know how I loved Casey. And I believe Casey is in heaven today. Now, don't you cry ... I saw you wipe the tears. But I just want to tell you this for your consolation. You know, Casey would come stay many weekends with Lucy. Lucy would be picking me up to take me to church after the boys left. Well, I'd be ready. I try to be ready when anybody is going to pick me up. My going is by somebody picking me up. Well, when I'd walk out there, Casey would always be in the back. Her little face, you know, would be there. We didn't have any classes downstairs, so Casey always stayed upstairs. But Casey listened closely every Sunday to the Sunday School lesson. She loved to go to church. Now that's consolation to you. I don't know how long she came; maybe you all were going to Kern Methodist. But one Sunday after Sunday School was over, we went on to the car. Well, sometimes Lucy stands and talks to Imogene or something. I just always go and get in the car. Well, Casey did too. Most of the time she did. So one Sunday she said, "Miss Whitus, I got saved." I said, "You did? Well, where?" She told me she'd been going to seems like it's a young people's little ministry or something. I said, "Casey, I am so glad," because you know I just loved her like I did you all. And I just complimented her. I said, "I am so happy, and I am so glad." And you know, I've just thought about it. I really believe she was saved. And I believe she's in heaven.

Of course you know on the Bible there's been so many books written – it's always been on the best-selling list – and there's a lot of things we don't understand. But I have heard some preachers say they believe that saved people, we'll know. A lot of questions have been asked Billy Graham, you know, about that.

Miss Whitus, thank you.

THE TOWN LIBRARY

The first I heard about the librarian's job, we were having an Eastern Star meeting, and Bob Evans got up and said, "There was a woman in through here the other day that said she could get some money that was left over from something during the war. All of these counties that didn't have a library in the town, she was going to get that money and set up some libraries." Well, so they talked a little bit, and they said, "Well, Mrs. Lucy Alderson or Mrs. Willie Barger would be good." When I first came here, Miss Lucy was the head of everything because she had a little more education and taught school. Mrs. Barger was a substitute teacher when I came here. From the time I heard Bob mention it, I thought, "Oh, I know I would love that" – because I used to read a lot. Well, Mrs. Barger's the one that got the job.

Mrs. Barger had the library first, and then she asked me one day, said, "Alice, I'm going to give that job up. Would you like to have it?" I had just found out that I was pregnant with another child. Thomas was nearly seven years old. I never did think about working. Well, the main woman, Mrs. Sudduth, came across over here then and asked me, said, "Mrs. Barger recommended you for librarian down there. Are you interested?" Well, I was. But I told the woman, I said, "Well, I think I'm pregnant. I'm not for sure. I couldn't work long, but I would love to be a librarian or just work with books." She said, "You go ahead and take this job. We've got a girl that hasn't been married too long working in our office, and she's expecting her first child, and she's going to work until she gets disabled to work." I said, "Well, ok."

I worked till August and quit to have Bobby. He was born the 5th of September, 1954. Oma Armes took my place for one or two weeks. Then Blanche Armes thought she wanted it. Blanche liked to read. She had it about a month – not over two months – and she went to Dr. Bowman with a problem of some kind and found out she had cancer. So she gave the job up.

They came back and asked me. So I told Tommy then, I said, "They've asked me to take that job." Bobby was about two months old or three, so it must have been close to December 1954. Tommy was on second shift. I said, "Now, I can't take the baby down there and work. You have your work clothes on. I can get here in 10 minutes. You can be ready to go." So it worked out until the next summer. I had my hours fixed. I worked two hours, two days a week. I think my days were Thursday and Friday, two to four in the afternoon, I believe. Well, the county would get a little more money, so it would go from two days to three. But I had my hours all together. Twenty-eight dollars a month. But that didn't make any difference. I worked for the thrill of working. Later on when there was minimum wage, we got minimum wage. We were getting a little more. I've forgotten what I worked for.

That was next to the best education that I ever had because I could see well and I could read a lot. One day somebody came to the library, a nearly grown person, they looked around, and they said, "Well, Miss Whitus, I guess you've read every book in this library." I said, "Well, you'd be surprised how many I've read and how many I haven't read." That's all I said about it.

Alice in the town library where she worked for 45 years.

But, oh, the more they liked to read, the better I liked to work with them and get those books. Of course school kids came down to the library. Mr. Hennessee knew the value of reading, and he would let his whole room come down at one time. Miss Imogene, I believe, had the second or third grade, and she always let her kids come to the library. That was their play period and all of them would come down there.

I never had one of those children to sass me in any way, because I treated them like human beings. And right today, if I go to the post office, I'll meet up with two or three of them and they just grab me and hug me. Oh, there's a few times that I'd just like to have busted their little butts sometimes when they'd lose books. One little girl had a big old dog that got ahold of a book and just tore pages, tore pages. Well, she brought it in and told me about it. I could have made her pay for it, but I didn't. I set that book where those pages were torn up on a high shelf where everybody could see it. I thought that would do more good than anything else.

In the beginning the Clinch-Powell book mobile brought books to us once a month. We didn't get many from our favorite authors. I knew what the people wanted to read; we all soon found out because they'd ask for certain books. Zane Grey and Grace Livingston Hill were the favorites. I just fell in love with Zane Grey. It's the wording that made his books so interesting.

The fine was three cents a library day that books were kept out. It was high school kids that would leave their books at school, sometimes going on two or three weeks. Well, I'd have to ask them to bring them back. One lady told me later, "Alice, I slipped through that door many times" – the shelves came right up to the door – "and put my book back. I'd leave it out at school in my locker and it would be a couple of weeks I'd forget to bring it home. On weekends I'd bring it here. I'd come to that door, maybe you were with someone, and I'd just slip it back." Well, later, somebody would want to check the book out, and then the card, well, I'd go to my file and there was the card.

I worked 45 years in the library. I retired in 1999. The town had a reception for me. It was just more than I would ever have expected. They had a big corsage for me. They fixed a book of pictures of the people that were down there. The town did it. I've got sacks in there of just little things, little booklets and things. They had a little money bag. The county gave me a plaque.

WIDOWHOOD

Miss Whitus has been a widow since 1972.

Tommy went to work at 16 years of age in the mines. One day I went to the post office and there was a card in there. It said, "Mr. Whitus, contact your health department in your county. We found something wrong with your lungs." Well, I just figured that was tuberculosis. Cancer was hardly known at that time. Seems like the men didn't have cancer of the lungs very often. Well, he went out there and they made another x-ray and said, "Go see your family doctor." Well, Tommy didn't have a family doctor. He hated doctors. He'd buy over-the-counter medicine, but it didn't help his trouble. So they made an appointment with a doctor in Knoxville. He said, "Yes, there is something wrong with your lungs, but it is not tuberculosis. You need to go in the hospital and let me treat you to see exactly what it is."

Oh, that black lung – he'd have to raise up in the bed to get his breath many, many nights. And he had to keep two or three of those breathers. It got so bad.

Tommy died in 1972. His intestines had burst and his stomach was filling up with fluid – poison. Peritonitis had set up and antibiotics would not kill it out. He was in so much pain. One time he said, "Alice, nothing but death is going to stop this pain." He stayed in intensive care three weeks before he passed away. Tommy's sisters and brothers and all of us were over there.

TODAY

Although she doesn't cook as often now as she once did, Miss Whitus' reputation as a great cook is well-deserved. Her family, plus anyone who ever had an opportunity to share one of the dinners held regularly at the Methodist church, can attest to her culinary skills. Ask anyone: "Who makes the best chicken and dumplings?" The answer will always be "Alice Whitus."

She told me, though, that one of her own favorite foods is kraut. She says it's good for the body.

The best day in the world and the best eating is a cold day and cooked kraut. I wanted to put some cabbage out there, but I'm going to buy some and make a can of kraut or two. I like it. I gather my cabbage heads in the early morning while they're firm. The night air makes them firm and cold. The cabbage needs to be cold. If you don't, you're going to have limp leaves in kraut.

And if you have a problem with kraut turning dark, she recommends putting a tablespoon and a teaspoon of vinegar on top of the cabbage before adding water to the jar.

Alice surrounded by garden. She has always had a green thumb.

Miss Whitus still makes a small garden, even though she celebrated her 90th birthday this year. She showed me squash, lettuce, onions and tomatoes on one of my recent visits. And she is still active in her community.

Polly got me to join the Home Demonstration Club when Thomas was a baby. We met then in a little chapel at the prison. I'm a past matron of the Eastern Star. I've had every one of the star points. I was president of the PTA. I just recently retired as president of the Senior Citizens. I have been president of every organization in Petros.

I never could remember scripture like I wanted to, like my daddy. He always quoted a scripture about "give until the bushel basket is full and then let it run over." That's like giving, helping your community.

I think Miss Whitus' papa would be proud.

Alice celebrating her 90th birthday.

LUCY ALICE DUNCAN PATRICK

FAMILY

John Duncan was of Scotch-Irish descent. His grandparents came to Tennessee from North Carolina. John, his parents, Wiley and Abigail Wilson Duncan, and his siblings – Tilda, Clarssie, Susan, Mary Ann (called "Polly"), Abby, Houston and William – lived in Scott County before settling in Morgan County. On January 1, 1900, John married Mary Leopper, and they had three children: Annie, George and Mary. The children died as infants. Mary, John's wife, died in 1906, a few days after giving birth to their third child.

Annie Engert's parents, Frederick and Augusta Engert, came to Morgan County, Tennessee, from Germany. Annie and her younger siblings – twins Lena and Clara, Rosa, Martha, William and Charlie – were the first generation of her family born in the Wartburg area. As a young woman, Annie worked in a boarding house in Petros that was owned by Sam and Nellie Joyner. Annie married John Joyner, Sam Joyner's brother. Annie and John had two children: Johney and Maudie. Johney died when he was a baby, and then John died a few years later. Annie kept boarders in the home she owned in Petros.

John Duncan was a widower, and Annie Engert Joyner was a widow with a little daughter when they married and started another family – a family that includes Lucy. This is Lucy's (my mom's) story.

Lucy.

I suppose I was born in the house I lived in until I got married, in Petros, Tennessee. Dr. Eblen might have delivered me when I was a baby. I don't know. My father was John Kimbrel Duncan, and my mother was Annie Amaline Engert Duncan. My dad was a big man. He was about 6'2" or 6'3". A little on the heavy side. He wasn't fat; he was just big. He had the prettiest white hair and a handlebar mustache. He had gray eyes. Beautiful gray eyes. I thought he was a good-looking man. He had a soft voice. He had a temper, but he didn't show it too often. My mother was fairly tall. She was about 5'6" or 5'7" or something like that. Just average size. I remember when she had black hair. And she had brown eyes. I thought Mama was a pretty woman too.

My dad was 55 years old when I was born, and Mama was 42. They were kind of old – I've always heard you take a chance on having children in your old age – but I think I turned out all right.

Mama had been married to John Joyner and they had two children. One of her children had died, and she had her daughter Maudie yet. After John Joyner died, she married my dad. They lived in the house where I was born.

No doubt Dad probably built that house. I think it started out maybe with three rooms and they built two more on. All the rooms were big, and we had a big back porch and then a "side porch" we called it. That was all Dad's land out through there. He had quite a bit of land. That old house that he lived in had beautiful wood in it when it was torn down. It had big old cedar wood. Actually the house was just about as good when it was torn down as some of them are now when they're built. The front porch was kind of kitty-cornered. There was a cellar underneath the house and a huge cherry tree in the front yard. Apple trees and pear trees and peach trees and cherry trees – big fields all up through there. Where all those houses are now *[Joe Duncan's house and the surrounding houses]* was part of our garden and fields.

I had three brothers. John Richard was the oldest. He was born the 26th of October, 1908. He had diphtheria when he was a baby, and I think that was what caused him to be slightly I guess you'd say retarded. He wasn't born that way. It was the diphtheria that caused it. But he knew what he was doing. He could do things. He could read, write. But he stuttered, and that would aggravate him. He'd start trying to tell something and he stuttered. Of course, when he was young – you know how kids will laugh at others and make fun. Diphtheria was a dangerous disease. In fact, people died from it back in those days. *[Diphtheria is an infectious disease of childhood that attacks the throat and heart. This infection is rare in the U.S. today because it is part of the DPT vaccine given to infants.]*

Lawrence Henry was born September 5, 1912. Lawrence was an athletic person. He always played basketball. When he was in high school, he was their center and he played all the time. I guess Lawrence was the smartest one of us four kids. He was salutatorian of his class. He worked all the time. He was always doing something. Mama depended on him, I suppose, more than any of us.

Lucy with brothers Richard, Lawrence and Leonard.

William Leonard was born January 31, 1917. We were closer because there was just two-and-a-half years between us in age. He was just my buddy, I guess. Leonard was a fun-loving person. He was like me; he got out of a lot of jobs if he could.

Then I came along July the 15th, 1919. I was just a normal person. Stayed at home and enjoyed ordinary things.

I also had a half-sister. Her name was Maude Ernestine Joyner. She was married before I was ever born. Maudie had married Ona Claiborne, and they had four girls and three boys.

I didn't know any of my grandparents. They had all died before I was born.

My parents were farmers. They grew just whatever farmers grow, and they had cows and hogs and chickens. Mama sold milk. We had a decent living, like most everybody did. Not rich or poor. I can remember I never would learn how to milk a cow because I knew if I did, I'd have to keep it up. So I never did learn how to milk a cow. I would help plant. I'd drop the corn or beans or set out potato slips or tomato plants or something. But I never could please my mama hoeing, so I got out of that job pretty easy. She was very particular, and she wanted things done right. You know, kids don't care sometimes, just so they get done. When it came to hoeing, no, I didn't.

Lucy and her brother Leonard.

Mama sold stuff on the farm. She'd expect us to use the cull beans, ones that had little specks on them or bug holes or something that we'd cut out, and she'd sell the others. I can remember me and my brother Leonard when we'd have to string some to cook, we'd get those good beans and cut little hunks out of them and make her think that we were using the cull beans. But she got with us. She knew what we were doing. So we didn't do it too much.

After I was old enough, I did all the housework. Mama would rather work outside. She loved outside work, and I didn't. So I would do the housework. Our house was five rooms. Back then, the rooms were big. You know houses now, two rooms would probably make one back then. We had three bedrooms and a big kitchen and a dining area. We didn't have living rooms back then. You just had your bedrooms in the "front room" we called it. We usually went to bed by dark – more or less good dark – and got up before daylight. Well, Mama would always get up early and she and some of them would go milk. I would wash the breakfast dishes and make the beds up and do things like that.

Mama did all the cooking until I was old enough to help her. I didn't start doing the main cooking for a long, long time. My family always ate a big breakfast. We'd usually have ham and eggs or bacon and eggs or oatmeal. If the chickens didn't lay much, we would have oatmeal or something besides eggs. Even back then we had cornflakes. We didn't have beef cows or anything like that. We raised our own pork. It was always ham or shoulder meat or bacon or backbones and ribs or sausage or something like that. We had that for breakfast. And of course we always had plenty of milk and butter.

We'd dry apples – peel apples and lay them on top of the cellar and dry them. We'd dry a lot of apples. And dry beans. Can stuff too. We didn't have freezers, so it was either can it or dry it. And Mama and Dad loved wine. They would make wine and cider. I can remember we had a cider mill. We'd get apples and grind them up and make cider. And then seems like they would make plum wine. But they did – Mama and Dad both loved the taste of wine. But none of us kids liked it.

We more or less ate together. We had a big, long table in the dining room. We had a bench behind the table, and then on the other side we had chairs. Chairs on the end. But the back of the table was a bench. That way, when you had company, you always had plenty of room to sit and eat. I always sat behind the table on the bench. Seems like Mama sat on one end and Dad sat on the other end, and then the kids sat on either side. And we'd always leave the food on the table. You kids get after me now for not putting everything in the refrigerator, but we would leave the stuff on the table. We had a tablecloth. We'd always spread something over it. It never sat out where the flies or anything would get on it. When you got ready for your next meal, whatever was left, you'd add to it.

Everybody usually came in and ate lunch at the same time. While they'd be working outside – and I was big enough – I would cook something at dinnertime, and lots of times we'd just eat leftovers at suppertime. My favorite foods were fried chicken and gravy and biscuits. Scrambled eggs. Boiled custard. Mama would make that big old pan full of boiled custard. Mama would go out and run a chicken down, a little frying chicken. We'd always have them fenced in. I can remember that I would always help – but I would never catch them. I was afraid of them because they'd flog me or something. Mama would take them and wring their head off and then stick them down in hot water and pick the feathers off. Then she'd cut them up and wash them real good and fry them. Good food.

The same way with killing hogs. You'd have all of that to do too. They did that at the house. Of course, as I said, I got out of all that stuff. It didn't appeal to me too much. I was inside washing dishes and frying something or other for them to eat. You'd always wait till it was real, real cold weather to kill the hogs because we didn't have refrigeration then. They would always kill them when it was cold weather. We had a big old long trough, and they salted down the meat real good and let it lay in that trough a certain amount of time. Then we had what we called a "smokehouse," and they would hang the hams and the shoulders and the middlings on some kind of a pole. Some way or other they'd fix it. That's the way you would fix meat. That's what I wonder now; I would be afraid to eat meat that's sat out, unless it was refrigerated. We didn't have that refrigeration back then. And nobody died from it. Don't ask me why.

I wondered aloud whether anybody in the family had high cholesterol.

I don't know. We never heard of that, honey. We didn't know what high cholesterol was. That's just something that's happened here lately. I'm sure people did, because they ate fat meat and they ate lard. But some people have it, and some don't. As far as I know, I'm the only one in my family that had high cholesterol. Of course I didn't know that until I was in my 70s. Mama was always in good health. She died from a stroke when she was 80.

I think we got our first electricity in 1936. I was probably in high school. I remember we would have two lamps burning. I thought that was a good light to study by. Our neighbor had electricity, and she'd say, "Well, how in the world can you see?" I don't know why we didn't have electricity, but evidently we got it the first chance we could. I remember that. We got a refrigerator then and an electric iron and washing machine – which was nice, considering everything. People used to wash on a wash board and boil their clothes in a kettle so they'd be nice and white and hang them on a clothesline. Then you'd heat your irons on a stove that had fire in it. Of course every time you'd have to clean the bottom before you'd start ironing or you'd get your clothes dirty. It's a life to look back to; I wouldn't want to have it again though. Not really.

When I asked my mom if she stayed busy from sunup to sundown, she replied . . .

Not really. People that were real smart probably did. I did my job, but I didn't stay busy all the time. I read a lot. I liked to read. Still do.

You know, back when I was growing up, there weren't that many things to do. Your neighbors would just get together and you'd play ball in the yard or in the field. More or less people worked. When you live on a farm, there's a lot of work to farming. It's a healthy life, but it's a hard life too.

Aunt Polly, my dad's sister, lived with us for a long time. Leonard and I were very mischievous children, from what I can hear. Bless her heart, she left and went to live with Uncle Bill Duncan at Oakdale. I can remember when I was a little old kid, crawling under her bed and when she'd go to bed I'd push it up. She never did marry. She said, "When I was young enough, I didn't want to get married because I didn't want any children. And then when I got older, I just didn't even want to get married." So, no, she was an old maid. But she actually was my favorite aunt. I loved her. She was probably about 85 when she died. She was living in Oakdale. But she would come every fall and stay with us for about a month.

Then Aunt Tildie, she lived in Petros, and she had a whole bunch of kids. About 10 or 11 or 12 of them. I know she would come to our house and spend the night. I just remember her and Aunt Polly being at the house. Of course Uncle Houston Duncan lived just a little piece from where we did. We'd visit a lot. He had a big family too.

How did the family celebrate holidays?

My mama would always cook us a good meal on our birthdays. Whatever we wanted. That was usually fried chicken. I knew it was a special day. I guess I got something for my birthday. I don't remember ever needing anything that I didn't get. On Thanksgiving, Mama would always – usually back then it was chicken – make chicken and noodles and all that good stuff. My mama was a good cook, and she'd make her own recipes up. My favorite thing she made was jelly rolls. She could make the best jelly rolls. And cakes and pies. Christmas was more or less just family get-togethers. Just something like it would be now. I remember we put a Christmas tree up every once in awhile, but not too often. We'd go to the woods somewhere and cut a tree down. I'm sure we put something on it, but it wasn't lights. I know we didn't have lights on our tree, but I don't remember what we put on it. Tinsel or something like that probably. And roping. We always had a Christmas program at the church house.

When I asked if she and her family believed in Santa Claus or whether that was something that was talked about then, she responded . . .

No, not really. We didn't pretend, I guess.

We always went to church on Easter. We colored eggs with the hulls off of onions. Mama would put the hulls in a pan and boil them, then put the eggs in there. That would make a beautiful maroon-colored egg. They were pretty. Of course there was egg dye back then, but you would use a lot of things that you had on hand without buying stuff.

The first car we had was a 1927 model Dodge. I can remember that car. Until we got a car, we would walk to church and wherever we went. Lawrence drove the car. He was probably 17, 18 – something like that. Mama, Dad and Richard never did learn to drive. I think I started learning how to drive when I was 15. My brother Lawrence taught me how to drive, and I got my license when I was 16 years old.

Mama and Dad bought cars. Not too many people had cars back then. They had a wagon probably. I remember we had a wagon, but I don't ever remember going anywhere. And seems like Dad had some kind of a buggy. But I just don't remember us going anywhere like to the store or anything. Somebody had cars back then before we did, I'm sure, because you had to get to a doctor or something.

The shift was down in the floor then. It was a thing with a knob on it where you'd move it up and down. The first car we had with a gear shift on the column was a 1936 model, I believe. Then eventually, after you got used to shifting gears, you got the automatic. But we still, even after I was married, we had a truck that we shifted gears on the column. I loved it. I loved driving. I wasn't afraid back then. I'm kind of skittish now about going places and doing things, but I wasn't afraid to drive back then, no, night or day either one.

I know one year Dr. Carr – Dr. Carr was a big politician too – asked me if I wanted to drive his car and go and haul some voters. Well, Imogene Langley and Jessie Duncan and I rode around. We'd go see if anybody wanted to vote. I know Leonard, my brother, said, "My goodness, that little old car, already three of you in there, how were you going to haul many voters?" And I said, "Well, we didn't care whether we got voters or not. We were just out running around." But I remember driving Dr. Jim's car to haul voters. He was one that was in politics. He never did run for anything, I don't think, but anyhow he was in politics.

I asked Mom if her parents let her take the family car out by herself. She said not very often, and then she told me about this adventure:

I know one time I asked Mama if I could have the car, and she said yes. When I got ready to start the car, it wouldn't start. Then I heard Lawrence decided I didn't need to go wherever I was wanting to go, and he did something so the car wouldn't start. I don't know what he did. He pulled a wire loose or something. Well, Anne and Peg and I just walked to where we were going. I went anyway. Yes.

After I pressed her, Mom admitted that they walked across the mountain – a good six miles of mountain road – to go to a ball game.

And I can remember one time Anne Claiborne and Leonard's first wife Mary, we walked to Coalfield. Coming back up the mountain, there were icicles hanging everywhere, so somebody gave us a ride. We walked way down there just to be walking.

CHILDHOOD MEMORIES AND SCHOOLING

We had eight grades in Petros. Then when I was in high school, I had to ride a school bus to Wartburg. In elementary school we walked to school. I lived about a half-mile from school. The school was on the hill where I live now. Back then children would walk a mile-and-a-half or two miles to school, where now they have to be picked up at their door. We would start school in August, and it was usually out in April or May. We walked in the wintertime too. It was daylight when we headed out to school. I don't remember what time, but I know it was always daylight. We never did walk either way in the dark. Whoever lived in the neighborhood, you'd always walk together. Richard and Lawrence were quite a bit older than me, so I don't ever remember going to school with them. You'd never be by yourself. I remember Reba Wilson walked to school with us. She was about my age. Then my brother Leonard had a bicycle. We would ride on his bicycle to school a lot of times. I remember a dog ran out one day and turned us over and really skinned my knees up. In fact, I still have scars from that fall. That dog hit us and knocked us over. The people that owned the dog came out, and, oh, they were cleaning my knees off and feeling sorry for me. Leonard kind of – he said, "Well, the old dog hit us, didn't it?" or something like that.

When I went to high school, the bus that I rode didn't have a heater on it. It wasn't such a pleasant job even riding a school bus in the wintertime. The bus picked me up in front of my house. I didn't have to walk to get on the bus. We must have been on central standard time, because I would leave for school seems like about 15 till seven of the morning. We rode the bus to Wartburg, and then our bus would have to go on to Gobey to pick up a load of kids. In the afternoon we would wait till they delivered the kids to Gobey to come home. So it was close to dark when we'd get home. I finished high school, and I didn't go on any further. I graduated in 1936.

When I asked my mom what subjects she studied in elementary school, she reminded me: "You're asking me about something that happened over 75 years ago!"

I guess it was just the basic studies, like English and reading and arithmetic and geography and history. I remember all my teachers. We had the primer – it was called primer then – and first grade. A Miss Smith was my first grade teacher. Ruby Joyner was my second grade teacher. Thelma Collins was my third grade teacher. Fourth grade I had Eva Summers; she married an Adcock. I had Aileen Slaughter my fifth and sixth grade. She would teach two grades. Seventh grade was a man named Judson Taylor. He was the Baptist church pastor. Then in the eighth grade was – one of my favorite people – Mr. Ed Bonifacius. I was afraid of him, but he was one of the best teachers I think I've ever had. He expected you to get your lessons. No foolishness. That's the kind of teacher I think we need. Somebody that's interested in the kids and wants them to learn. And we did. We got our lessons.

Every day when I was in elementary school, we would march down in the auditorium and have chapel. I don't remember who – the principal probably – read the scripture. We'd have a song and a prayer, and then we'd march back to our rooms. We had that every day.

Hardly any of the teachers had a college degree. I remember later, in wartime, some of the teachers just had a high school education and they let them teach because so many of the regular teachers went somewhere else to work because they made more money in the plants. I know one teacher went over to Oak Ridge and worked as a chauffeur. Then when she got through doing that, she went back to teaching.

Subjects in high school? Freshman year was home economics and civics and English and algebra. And then the second year was some kind of history. History was my favorite subject. I always loved history. We had to have English four years, history four years, science two years, and a foreign language two years. I took French. I can remember a few things. Home economics was a four-year thing. Then our phys ed classes, we didn't have a certain time for them because we'd go outside and play ball or jump rope or something like that. At our lunch hour, we would just go outside and just walk up and down the walk and probably play ball. There wasn't that much to do. I think they had a little merry-go-round kids could get on.

We had basketball teams and softball teams. Football. I was on the high school girls softball team. Oakdale, Sunbright and Wartburg were the only places we played softball. I played left field. I always did like ball games. But I didn't play basketball because you had to stay and practice after school, and I didn't have a way from school to Petros. So I didn't go out for basketball. We practiced softball at lunchtime. For uniforms, I think we had some "rejects" from the basketball team. Seems like we did. Probably shorts and a top or the long pants.

I know we went to Harriman to play a ball game one evening and we rode in the back of a truck. The boys and girls teams rode in there. We had to go down there to play Oakdale. That was fun. We didn't use gloves. We just caught the ball with our hands. Just the pitcher and catcher and first baseman had gloves. The catcher would have a mitt, and the pitcher and first baseman had gloves. But the rest of the players just played without gloves. I don't know how we caught the ball, but we did – most of the time.

Our coach was one of the teachers that taught – the science teacher always – which was Mr. Potter or Mr. Knisley. One of them was our coach. I don't think we had a lady coach. Just a man. Times have changed so much. But we were the "Central Bulldogs" even then, and our colors were blue and white.

The high school that I went to sat where the old Wartburg Elementary School used to be, right in the middle of Wartburg. It burned down maybe two or three years after I was out of school. Some of the kids went to Coalfield and some went to Oakdale until they got a new schoolhouse built. But now they have a different schoolhouse from what was rebuilt then. In fact, it's much larger because so many more kids go.

There were 28 kids in my graduating class. There were, I believe, six girls from Petros who went on to high school and completed it: Geneva Stewart and Dorothy Ashley and Susie Tucker and Pauline Beene and Emma Kennedy and me. And then out the road was Joann Barger. Most of the others were from around Lancing or Gobey or Wartburg or somewhere. None of the boys in my eighth grade class went on to high school. I don't know what happened, but they didn't.

My best friends were Anne and Zona Claiborne. And then there was an Anna Mae Brooks, the preacher's daughter. Later on, the Scarbroughs – Helen and Leo and Marie – were friends. Louise Williams – she was Louise Hampton back then – was my best friend in high school. There's still several of our class living, but a lot have died. I guess I'm the only one here in Petros now.

We took our lunch to school. Elementary school didn't have a cafeteria, but in high school they had a cafeteria and you could eat

Mary Bradshaw, Lucy Duncan and Anne Claiborne wearing shorts in the snow. Outbuildings at the Duncan homeplace are in background.

there. It cost you less than a dollar. Always less than a dollar – 15 or 20 cents or something or other. Or you could take your lunch. Whatever you wanted to do.

On dates, we went to movies at the Princess Theater in Harriman. I don't remember doing anything else really but walking home from church or something like that. Boys would walk me home. I don't know – I wasn't ashamed of the house, but I wasn't proud of the way it looked either. I know in wintertime we always had sweet potatoes in the front room there. You'd raise stuff and you'd have to take care of it. And there'd be barrels – Mom and Dad would put barrels of sweet potatoes there in the front room where the fire was, and there were those blamed-ole sweet potatoes! I didn't want anybody to come. I didn't. It wasn't that the house was dirty; I was just, you know, I wasn't proud of it.

Lucy in front of her homeplace.

I wanted to be a nurse when I grew up – until my brother had a motorcycle wreck. When he had a motorcycle wreck and I had to feed him and see blood oozing out of his bandages – I changed my mind real quick. I would probably have had to go to Knoxville for nursing school. It would have been a hospital in Knoxville. Probably General Hospital. There wasn't a hospital in Oak Ridge; in fact, Oak Ridge wasn't thought of then. Two of my friends, Leo and Helen Scarbrough, made nurses.

EMPLOYMENT

I started working in Oak Ridge in April of 1943. I started out with a surveying crew, and we were outside all day. I was really suntanned. We wore pants – usually jeans or something – and my face and arms would be brown. Imogene Langley and I went over to the personnel office on a Wednesday to put our applications in. The personnel office was on what's the main turnpike now. They told us to come to work on Friday, or we could go to work the next day. We asked if we could wait till Monday. We were on a surveying crew. That's what they put us to. Really, back then, it was either secretarial work or canteen work or the surveyors. And of course we'd rather had the surveyor job as to have that canteen work. And we weren't secretaries.

We worked for Stone & Webster. They had "party chiefs" they called them. We had one guy that was a party chief, and then two were something else. One guy carried a transit and would read things. Then they had another instrument, a level. The girls always held a "plumb bob" they called it. You'd dangle it, and you'd have to get it exact when we were surveying out railroads. That's what we did – surveyed out the railroads. And we would do that. Then they had a big old long metal thing and we'd have to carry chains. We called it the "chain." When we'd get through at night, we'd have to flip it and make it go in the thing. It was interesting work. It was fun.

One of the guys was from Pennsylvania, and he cussed. Oh, he cussed – it was awful – when we were surveyors. After awhile somebody complained about it, him a cussing so much in front – there were four girls in our crew and probably four men and the party chief – but somebody complained and they got rid of him and we had somebody else.

We surveyed around all of those railroads. We were out in Y-12 quite a bit too. Everywhere. I can remember we were just among those bulldozers and pans and things. Machinery was going all the time. And it was woods then. In fact, I got chiggers all over me one time. I worked with the surveyors about four or five months. All during the hot summer. But then, after awhile, one of the guys that was over that wanted me to drive him. They had chauffeurs that would drive the bosses around. Well, I would dearly love that job. I drove till the weather got real cold. When the weather got cold, it got kind of cold to sit in a car and wait on somebody or something so I started working in the office. There were about, oh, I'd say 10 or 11 girls in one great big room, and we kept account of all the stone that was hauled. I was working at that when I quit in September 1944.

Where Dr. Casey's and Dr. Bridgeman's offices are today in Oak Ridge is where our office was. It was somebody's house, and then they built a big old long building on it to make offices. That's where the blueprint office was. The engineers drew up plans and everything. They were in one end of the building, and we were in the other side of it. I know there was a railroad then, but I don't know whether it's still there or not.

I had some good friends over there. I know when we were working in this office, one of the girls lived in Knoxville. Gladys was her name. We all went home with her one night and spent the night and went to one of those S&W Cafeterias and ate our supper. Most of the girls were from somewhere else. Some came from Missouri and some from Texas and just all different places. Some were Yankees and had that Northern talk. There was a Betty Lambert I remember. She and her husband had a trailer outside of the gate and they had one child. I can just see her now. I just remember her talking about her little boy. I don't know whether she had him with her or not. She might have left him back with her parents. There was one girl that lived in Lenoir City. Bossy. Oh, lord, she was bossy. She'd try to tell everybody what to do. Then I know we had another girl, a real pretty girl, but I don't remember her name. She stayed in the lounge three-fourths of the time. Well, after awhile the girl that was in charge in our room said, "I'm getting tired of this. It's not fair to you others for her not to do anything." So she told the boss, and he fired her. Just little old things.

I know the boss had asked me when we started working if I would take that office manager job, and I said, "How much more is it going to pay?" He said, "Five dollars a week." I said, "I don't want it." I didn't because you had to watch everything, and I didn't want to make somebody mad. Just like this girl had to tell on the other one, you know, report her.

I made 62-and-a-half cents an hour when I was a surveyor. If we worked six days, I would clear $28. If we worked seven days, I cleared $35. That's little money – but it was money back then. I liked my job. A bus came to Petros. When I rode the bus, it cost $1.50 a week. A guy from Wartburg drove one of the buses, and Clyde Hensley drove a bus a long time. And then there was a bus that came from Fork Mountain. I rode that most of the time. It would leave over there way, way down Fork Mountain. I'd catch the bus at just about good daylight, hardly daylight, and get home about dark. Seems like about seven o'clock. We'd work 10 hours. I know that bus would be full when it would come by my house to get me. Some guy sat up in a seat, and when I got on, he gave me his seat and he'd sit on a bucket. He had a bucket up there next to the driver. I remember he'd sit in a seat till I got on, then he'd give me his seat and ride on that bucket.

Then after awhile we got a ride with a man who lived over there at Fork Mountain. Bell was his last name. He had a pretty good job. But, anyhow, Imogene Langley and Catherine Carson and Naomi Walls and Theda Hart's sister, Thelma Ruffner, – we rode. The three from Coalfield and me and Imogene from Petros. I think he charged us $1.50 a week to ride. I know two or three times for some reason he couldn't go to work, but he would bring his car and I would drive on in and pick them all up. Then when we'd get off at night, I'd park the car in front of the house and he'd come by and pick it up. I loved to drive then. I drove his car. But the thing of it is, these girls in Coalfield – they lived in Coalfield and he would let them off where the Snak-N-Pak is now. They would get off at that road and then walk on around to wherever they lived. Well, whenever I was driving I would take them home. And he could tell the difference. He'd check the mileage, I guess, and he could tell the different mileage. He never did say anything to me, but he knew I did.

The roads were gravel roads then. And dusty. I mean they were dusty. I know the buses would see who could get out first because when you hit down that road from Oliver Springs on to Petros, it was a gravel road. A dirty, dusty road. To drive from Petros to Oak Ridge took probably close to an hour, I guess.

I know whenever we would go to Knoxville, it was bumper-to-bumper. It would take you at least an hour, maybe an hour-and-a-half to get to Knoxville from Oak Ridge. See, everybody – anybody – could get a job then because there were so many. They had a laundry. And cafeterias – it didn't cost much; you could eat a good meal for a dollar. There were canteens everywhere where people could buy drinks or food or something. They just had so many different jobs. I think when my brother Leonard worked over there, he worked for a J.A. Jones Construction Company.

We didn't know what was going on in Oak Ridge. I had the least idea what it was. And, really, I didn't wonder that much about it. Some people let on like they knew what was going on, but I don't think anybody did – because they didn't complete each thing. One thing wasn't completed; you had just a part. We had a badge with our picture on it and our number. We had to wear that all the time. We went down in Y-12 a lot and we had a little old blue paper tag. It was just paper with a string, and we'd tie it around our badge.

I quit in September 1944 because I was going to go with your daddy, Woodrow Patrick. I told them why I was quitting, and they told me when I came back if I wanted a job to go to Tennessee Eastman and be rehired. But I didn't. I raised my family and didn't work again until 1977. Meryl Gunter asked me if I wanted to work in Gunter's store in Petros. So I worked in the store there from 1977 till 1995.

MARRIAGE AND CHILDREN

I have no idea how the Patricks ended up in Petros. Woodrow's mother – Eliza Litton Patrick – had brothers and sisters in Oneida, Tennessee. His dad – Ancil Patrick – had family in Kentucky. I was in high school, I guess, before they moved to Petros. The Patricks lived up on the hill – "Bungalow Hill" we always called it. It was a big old house made with a porch all the way around it. It had this dome roof to it. It was a company house. Woodrow, his brother Lawrence and their dad all worked for the Diamond Coal Company. They had worked at Fork

Mountain. When they came to Petros, the company let them have that house because they were a big family. They lived up there for quite awhile, and then they bought the other place where they lived when we got married.

Later, Mr. Patrick (Ancil) worked at Y-12. He worked for Stone & Webster. He was a carpenter foreman. He worked over there quite awhile during the wartime. When I was working over there, he was working there. In fact, I rode with John Barry some, and he rode in the same car. Mr. Patrick was called "Cedrick" because he liked to listen to *Lum and Abner* on the radio. Back then it was just radio; we didn't have TVs, just radio. He was always telling them something about it, and they started calling him "Cedrick." Cedrick was just a character on that radio program. Mr. Patrick was a good worker. He was a hard worker. He had to work. He raised a big family. Eight girls and two boys.

I knew Woodrow's sisters Ruth, Maxine and Helen. My dad died in 1941, and I can remember him from then. I don't remember when we started dating, but we got married in 1944. I do know that. We dated off and on more or less till he went in the Army. When he went in service, he asked me if I would wait for him. I told him I didn't know – because I just liked him then. But of course after he was in service, I reckon your heart grows fonder in absence, and we got engaged while he was still in service. When he came home in December 1943, he brought me an engagement ring. He was in for five or six days, and he had to go back. He was stationed in Louisiana. Then he came back home in July, and we got married the 4th of July, 1944.

You had to get a marriage license and a blood test back then. I know he got his before he left out of the Army coming home. You could go to Knoxville to some building there – I forget what it was called – and get a blood test and get your results the same day. I know me and this girl from work rode a bus, a work bus or something, from Oak Ridge to Knoxville, and I got my blood test and got the results back.

We got married at Woodrow's parents' home. Elmer Brown married us. We got married at nine o'clock on Tuesday night. I was working in Oak Ridge then, and I worked Tuesday daytime and got married at nine o'clock. I wore a white dress that had red polka-dots and a pair of slippers that you didn't have to have a stamp to buy. Back then they rationed everything, and maybe you got two stamps or three stamps a year or something like that to buy good shoes with. But you could go buy other types, sandals or something, that you didn't have to have a stamp to get. You couldn't really tell the difference. They were just a cheap shoe. I know Maudie Claiborne, my sister, had children then and they needed good slippers. By working over at Oak Ridge, I could get extra coupons and things. I would get them and give them to her to buy her children shoes with. But I remember I had those. They were white slippers.

Woodrow wore his uniform. Back then they had to wear their khakis. They had those khaki uniforms, the summer uniform. They had to wear them all the time. Now, if they come out they can wear civilian clothes. They weren't allowed to do that back then. Even when they were on furlough, they had to wear those Army clothes when they went anywhere. So he got married in that, yes. I guess all of Woodrow's family was there, but I didn't say anything to my family. I know Woodrow always said after that he was just so sorry that he didn't ask Mama to go. But I didn't ask any of them. I don't know. I've thought about that – why did I do that?

We were together about a week, and he had to go back to Louisiana. See, it was wartime then. I didn't see him any more until the latter part of September. He had got his orders; he was going overseas in October. So I went to Camp Polk, Louisiana.

His mother and I went together. We rode a bus. Mr. Patrick took us to Chattanooga, and we got on the bus at one-thirty in the evening. We got to Camp Polk, Louisiana, about nine o'clock the next night. That was a lot of bus-riding. We had layovers in Mississippi. Now you could make it in a lot less time, I suppose. They had a guest house, and we had a room there. His mother stayed two days. We got there on Friday night, and then she left to come back home on Sunday evening. She rode the bus back home by herself. She rode a long, long way just to stay for a short time. She just wanted to do that though.

I stayed there for five weeks until he left. Of course he was still there a day or two after I had come home. I didn't see him ship out. Another girl from Knoxville and I rode the train coming home, and we couldn't get a seat. I had my suitcase, and we put that suitcase down in the aisle. We sat on that suitcase and rode all night on that suitcase. De Ridder, Louisiana, is where we got on the train, and we rode to Knoxville.

I got pregnant then, and Pat was born July 9, 1945. Woodrow was in Czechoslovakia when Pat was born. I sent him a telegram. There was a depot in Petros, and you could send telegrams from there. His sister Faye went there and sent him a telegram and told him he had a little boy. It was wartime then, and they were fighting. He was in Germany, of course, and Czechoslovakia and several places. Pat was five months old before he ever saw him.

He was overseas from October 1944 until December 1945. It was December the 9th, 1945, when he came home. Pat was exactly five months old. He had his discharge when he came home because the war was over then. But he stayed in the reserves. He didn't talk too much about the war. No. He was rather nervous – very nervous – when he got back home. He said they would have to travel at night without the lights on. He was in the artillery. He said he could remember when it would be so cold they would put hay in the bottom of their boots to keep their feet from getting so cold. He had a rough time, so really I didn't ask him to relate all that to me. If he wanted me to know, he would tell me things. But I didn't ever ask him that I can remember. He didn't look too much different when he came home. No. I thought he looked good, of course.

I was living with Mama. We stayed there with her till we got us a place to live. My brother Leonard had a little log house, and he wasn't married, so he let us live in that house. I never will forget when we moved out, just a little piece from where Mama's house was, the next morning my brother Richard came to the house, and he said, "I've just come over here to see if Pat was all right." And I said, "Richard, I'll take care of him." He said, "I just wanted to see if he's all right."

Richard loved you kids. Pat and Bill would go to town with him when they were big enough – little old boys seven or eight years old or something like that, nine or ten. They'd always go to the store with him. Sit around with him. They enjoyed getting out and doing things too; they got away from me. And they would be with him. Every day, usually, they'd walk up to the store with him or something. He'd buy them a Fudgsicle or a drink or something.

We lived in Leonard's house about three years. Then when he got married, he wanted his house. So Mama gave us a piece of land, and we built us a little house and lived in it quite awhile. We had Gene Buxton build it. We just built a four-room house. The house cost $1,600 – if you can imagine building a four-room house for that now. It was just a living room and two bedrooms and a kitchen/dining room together. But we had room. And then as the family gradually added on, we built two more rooms to the house.

Woodrow went to work for Union Carbide at Y-12 in Oak Ridge in May 1948. He started out as a material handler. He was in the reserves, so in 1951 when the Korean War was started, they called him back. He had some good bosses, and they worked to help him – he was needed more outside than he was in the service. When they first called him back, he got a deferment for two-and-a-half months. We had two kids then. During that two-and-a-half months, if he'd had to go then, he would have been shipped to Korea. That's when they were fighting, and he would have been shipped to Korea. But that deferment that he had for two-and-a-half months kept him out. But then he had to go to North Carolina, Fort Bragg probably. Seems like he went in February and got out in May. He just had to stay in two-and-a-half months and he got out. And he got a discharge, a final discharge, that time. He didn't stay in the reserves.

I asked Mom to tell me about the births of us children.

Pat was born right there at my mama's house. Then when Bill was born on February 9, 1947, we lived in that log cabin of my brother's, and that's where he was born. I was at home with both of my babies. The doctor – Dr. Jim Carr – and my sister Maudie were there. She would help Dr. Carr with babies. Not just my babies, but everybody's. She would help him. She was more or less a midwife. I know when Bill was born, he was born sneezing. They gave that poor little fellow a dose of castor oil. I can remember that. That's what people gave you back then when anything was the matter with you. Castor oil. So Bill got a little dose of castor oil. He was born with a cold, I reckon. He was born sneezing. He weighed 10 pounds and 2 ounces. He was a pretty good-sized baby.

Mama made me stay in bed a week. Pat was born on a Monday morning at eight o'clock. I stayed in bed until the next Sunday and she let me get up. Bill was born on a Sunday morning around ten o'clock. It was in February, but it was pretty weather. It wasn't that cold. So I stayed in bed another week. Mama helped me with Pat and with Bill. She'd give them a bath and everything. When Bill was born, your daddy's sister Ruth stayed with us those days. But I think Mama would come over and give them their baths and take care of them.

I had no medicine when I had Pat and Bill. Not a thing. Dr. Carr was there about an hour before they were born. We called him when I first had my pains. I know when Pat was born, Dr. Carr lived at Oakdale and he was the prison doctor. So we called him, and he got there about one o'clock Monday morning. He said, "It's going to be a little while before that baby gets here, and I'm going up to the prison now and get me some sleep." So he went up there, and he came back to our house at seven o'clock. Then Pat was born at eight. He weighed six and three-fourths pounds.

When Bill was born, we called Dr. Carr on Sunday morning. He probably was at the house about that length of time again. I wasn't in labor all that long. You know, I got plenty of exercise. It wasn't fun, but it wasn't that bad.

With you and Gail, I was knocked out for about 10 minutes. You were born at Dr. Fred Stone's Clinic in Oliver Springs. The reason I went there was my sister-in-law had had her baby there, and she really liked it. She said, "Oh, they put you to sleep before the baby gets there and it takes those hardest pains away from you." I said, "That's where I'm going then." So that's where you were born. You fooled around longer getting here, I suppose, because we were at the doctor's office, or there at the clinic, at least six or seven hours before you were born. You arrived about three o'clock in the afternoon on June 5, 1952. You weighed nine pounds.

Lucy Patrick, ca. 1950.

I don't remember being too hot there at the clinic, but I can remember after I went back home, that was the hottest June I believe we've ever had. And we didn't have air-conditioning then either. We just had our windows open. Then when Gail was born, it was August, the first day of August, 1954, so it was still hot weather. We weren't used to air-conditioning, and something you're not used to, you don't miss. And the house was cool. We had fans. We had a fan in each end of the house. It would blow air through. So I made it ok. Gail weighed eight pounds when she was born.

Then when Linda, the last little one, came, I was 40 years old. I was too old to be having babies anyway. My water broke Thanksgiving, and I had to stay in bed for five weeks until she was born. She was due in January 1960, but she came the 23rd of December, 1959, and she just lived five days. She was born in Oak Ridge Hospital. Dr. Van Hook *[Stonewall Jackson Van Hook]* was the doctor, but she was born before my doctor got there. The two nurses delivered her. Within 30 minutes after I got to the hospital, the baby was there. She didn't fool around. I don't know what the problem was, but I said I was too old to have had a baby at my age anyway, so I've always wondered if that had anything to do with her not living. But she had a heart condition or something. Something was wrong, because when she died my doctor asked if I cared if they would do an autopsy to see what caused the death in case maybe it would help somebody else. So – I don't remember the exact terms, but he said the food couldn't get to her little body and she more or less starved to death. There was a tube stopped up somewhere. I would say now they know all that stuff. But that was back in 1959.

I don't remember choosing anybody's name, because I always said everything I chose a name for would die. Every calf we'd have, or pig, or dog, or cat or something I would name, they would die. I said, "I'm afraid to name a child." I don't know that I actually picked any of my children's names. Pat's a junior, after your dad. And your dad liked "Billy." Maudie, my sister, liked Dr. Carr, so Bill's name is "Billy Carr."

The boys, Pat and Bill, had a cousin in Clinton, June Dotson, that they really liked. That's why they wanted you named "June." I think your dad put the "Alice" to it because that was part of my name. Seems like Alma, my sister-in-law, picked out the "Wanda" part to Gail's name, and maybe your dad picked "Gail." You all got names, but I didn't name you. No.

I just remember that it hurt much worse to have girls than it did boys. Even if I was put to sleep at the last minute, I can still remember the pains that I had with the girls. I didn't stay in bed a week, but I did two or three days because I felt like it. Clara Vitatoe stayed with me when you were born. And then Joann Patrick stayed when Gail was born. Back in those days you stayed in bed if you could.

MEMORIES OF PETROS

This was a mining camp. They had a company store. And then besides the company store, there were three or four other stores. And we had an opera house where they'd have shows and things. Had a barbershop and a poolroom.

There were doctors in Petros. A Dr. Donaldson lived next to Alice Whitus' house. And then there was a Dr. Heacker that lived in Oliver Springs, and he'd come to Petros. Then after a bit, Dr. Carr from Oakdale had an office here in Petros. Doctors made house visits back then. When you needed to see the doctor, they'd go to your house.

Aunt Martha Taylor and Uncle Riley Taylor were two of the leading citizens in Petros. She was my mother's sister. They had a grocery store. Huldie Page had a restaurant right next to them. There were partitions; it was still the same building. And then there was a pool hall. Post office. A bank. Then on the other side of the street was a company store and doctor's office and a drugstore. Mrs. Quisenberry and her husband ran the drugstore. They sold medicine and ice cream and magazines and drinks and things like that. They had a little place with tables where you could go in and get a cone of ice cream and sit down and eat it or whatever. Then they had a porch with benches on it where people could sit out there and watch the traffic go by. After the Quisenberrys died, Ada Morton's daddy, Luther Morton, put a grocery store up in there. He had a grocery store and Ada had a beauty shop. She would do your hair. I think it was 75 cents to wash it and roll it and dry it and whatever.

Bernard Sexton, Lucy Duncan, Woodrow Patrick and Imogene Langley on the street in Petros, ca. 1941. The two-story building on the right is Quisenberry's drugstore, and the buildings on the left are Hulda Page's restaurant and Riley and Martha Taylor's grocery store.

Willie Barger used to have a little place, next to the Masonic Hall, that we called the "Rag Store." Somebody brought the stuff in. People bought a lot of their clothes there. She just sold clothes. Nice clothes. You could buy a coat for 50 cents or three dollars or something like that.

Seems like Seaborn Bradley ran the pool hall. I never was in it. Hix Morton had something; maybe Hix Morton had that pool hall. We had a barbershop. I remember the first haircut I got. Shirley Fairchilds, a man, had a barbershop and he cut my hair. I had long hair, and Mama would plait it up. I think I was probably in the fourth grade when she let me have it cut. And then I remember Frank Neal and his daughter had a barbershop and a beauty shop combined. That's when you would get a permanent and they'd put you on those old hot things and they'd hang down in that machine. It was a thing that stood on a stand and it had curlers on it. They'd clip them on, and they'd get hot. You'd have a frizzy permanent. You know how tight, tight permanents look now? Well, that's about what they all looked like back then. Unless they were careful, it would get too hot and burn you.

My brother Lawrence had a store in Petros, where the Baptist church parking lot is now. I don't remember when he had that, but it seems like he opened the one on the corner next to his and Mozell's house the year Mama died. 1957. He had probably been up there maybe two or three years. Lawrence worked in a mine. He didn't work *in* the mines; he worked on the outside of the mines. He hauled coal when he and Mozell got married. Then he had a truck that he would take to Knoxville on Fridays and haul stuff back to the stores for them to sell. Then he got that store up there. But I don't remember just when it was.

Elections used to be at Huldie Page's building all the time. She had a restaurant, and Huldie would always cook. Election workers, that's more or less about all they got then. Maybe two or three dollars. I think the first time I helped hold the election, I got $10. Dad used to help. He was a judge. He and Uncle Houston Duncan, I can remember they would help hold the elections. They closed the elections then at noon and then opened up at one. Well, Dad would come – I was just a little old kid – but Dad and the judges would come out to the house, and Mama had dinner cooked for them. Dad would put that election box on the middle of the bed. "Don't you touch that now." You know I wanted to, of course, but I didn't.

They closed the polls at four o'clock then. They were paper ballots. Whenever you started counting them, the clerk sat there, and it would take four or five hours to count the elections. I never did help then. They had machines when I started helping.

My mom lives on "Schoolhouse Hill" in Petros, two doors down from the Methodist church. Her home overlooks the town of Petros. The rock cliff that could have influenced the naming of the town is just below her house. At least three other homes sat on that same site, and all three burned, the most recent being my mother's house in 1996.

The first house must have been when my mother was a teenager, in the late 1800s. Sam and Nellie Joyner lived there with their family. They kept boarders, men that worked on the train and such. They fed them; probably did their clothes. My mother worked there. She was there day and night; she lived in the house. That house burned, but I don't know what caused it. Evidently they rebuilt the house, but I don't think it was a boarding house. Just a family. It was a big house. Had an upstairs and all to it.

The first people that I remember living there was one of the Joyner daughters, Mary, and her husband, Renfroe Evans. They had three children. When I was in the second grade, my school teacher stayed with them. So evidently they did keep more boarders. We would come to the gate and wait on our teacher and walk her to school. A bunch of kids would meet her every morning and walk to school with her.

Thelma Collins was her name. We would see who could hold her hand walking to school. I don't think we walked her home from school. We didn't have school buses. When school was out, we walked home. She was probably in her 20s. She was just a young lady. I can just remember us doing that.

Then the Charlie Walls family lived here a long time. I guess probably after they moved out, Ted Hyde's family moved in. I'm not really sure on that. When Ted Hyde's family lived here, their house burned the week of Christmas. The parents had their toys hidden upstairs, and they didn't get anything out. Just the other day, I was talking to one of the children *[Mona Justice]* who used to live here, and she said just what clothes she had on was all. She didn't have any shoes. I think she was just barefoot or maybe had socks on. It was a two-story house. It was a big house. She said they had two big stoves that heated the house – a stove in the kitchen part and a stove in probably the living room. She thought the fire probably started from the stove in the kitchen.

Then we built our house and moved in here the 11th of January, 1966. We bought this piece of property from Lawrence, my brother. We paid him $800 for it. A Mr. Scandlyn of Scandlyn Lumber Company from Harriman built the house. It was a good lot, but trees had grown up. He had that all cleared off and built the house. I think it cost us $14,000 – if you can imagine a house like that for $14,000. Then it burned on May 6, 1996. The lightning struck it, so I know what caused it. I just think if I could have – if I was at myself and done things different – but of course the smoke ran me out. I couldn't see. I just think if I could have started smothering that fire out – but I was trying to beat it out with my hands and couldn't. Then when I was going to get the water, I couldn't get back in, it was so smoky.

Mom's house was totally destroyed by the fire, and she lost all her possessions. Today, though, she's back on the same hill with the same good people as her neighbors. Life in Petros hums along within her sight.

Brushy Mountain Penitentiary, the main employer in town, is just two miles away.

My dad worked as a guard at Brushy Mountain Prison just a little bit. Not too much. He worked the night shift some. I know he said some prisoner would be on the guard shack with him.

Women who had husbands working there would go up there and eat their lunch on Sundays. They would always feed them. A lot of people didn't have cars, and they would walk. None of my family worked at the prison then so I never did go. I used to take Pat and Bill up there when they were little boys and get their hair cut. It was a prison barber; he was in prison. Of course they'd just shingle it off. Twenty-five cents. Anybody could go in, but they didn't take you behind the walls where the prison was. The barber was in the front there.

Used to, whenever a prisoner would escape, they had a whistle at the prison and it would start blowing. Then there at the last, however many long blows it would give, you would know that was how many prisoners were out. I would always make sure the car was locked and the doors were fastened. But one time when the old schoolhouse was up here, they had a group of people cleaning the schoolhouse. Four escaped prisoners came across the hill and stole some lady's car. They came and turned in my driveway here. Of course I didn't know who they were, but they were escaped prisoners and they had stolen this lady's car. She was working up there on this cleaning crew. But they caught them. They usually catch them pretty soon because, well, they're trained to do that. They know what to do. Know how to find them.

Well, there was a prisoner came through when I was just a kid. We always washed on Mondays. We hung the clothes out on the clothesline, and everything had gotten dry but Richard's overalls and they were still hanging on the line. Well, when I went out to get them, they weren't there. A prisoner had come through the yard and taken his overalls off the clothes line and went over in that lot, just about where Buddy Hall's house is, changed his clothes and went on out the road with those overalls on. Sure did. Came and took a pair of overalls off the clothesline. We didn't see him or anything.

Then another time, that man that got out and went down to Harriman and killed this woman, he came across the hill where we lived. He came right through our yard and went up the hill. Mama was sitting on the porch. She said he passed right by. He was carrying his shoes. He spoke to her and she spoke to him, and he went on out the front gate and went down through the field and went down Black Creek and on to Harriman. He killed a woman down there. They electrocuted him. *[That execution, carried out in 1960, was the last execution in Tennessee until 2000.]*

I remember a Mr. Blevins. He worked in an office up there. We could take our film and he'd develop the pictures. Wouldn't cost a thing. Of course I guess his workers did it, but he had it done. He was kind of an older man, and he limped. I can remember taking a lot of film up there, and he would develop the pictures for me.

Mr. Blevins and Mr. Cox went to get a load of prisoners. I don't remember where; I guess it was Kentucky. They called the cars that hauled the prisoners the "long chain." They stopped the long chain somewhere to eat, and the prisoners got them to take their handcuffs off. When they did, they got his gun. The prisoners killed Mr. Blevins and Mr. Cox too. They killed them both. They had stopped to eat, and see, they took their handcuffs off of them so they could eat. They were just being nice to them.

We had one guy that came up there as warden, and he started having all those houses on state property around the prison torn down. If you'll remember, there were a lot of nice homes at the state. I don't know what happened to that guy. He didn't stay there too long.

To get one of the houses at the state, you had to work there. Usually the warden and deputy warden and the higher-ups got the best houses. Maybe a guard would get a house sometimes. They had a commissary where they could buy groceries. Of course they would come down in Petros and trade, or we would go up there and trade if we wanted to. The commissary was on the road where you turn to go across the mountain. Just right on the corner there. A big old long building.

Back when everybody was getting polio vaccine – what was it called? Salk? – people could go up to the prison. I know all you kids were small, and we all went up to the prison and they gave us vaccine up there. That's where everybody went from Petros.

I can remember the day in 1972 the prison closed. They had buses coming in, hauling the prisoners out. Highway Patrol and the law were on every corner and everything. It didn't reopen until 1976.

CHURCH MEMORIES

We always went to church. My dad didn't go to church much, but Mama always went. And of course we would walk. We would walk a lot until I think I was maybe – how old was I? – maybe 10 or 11 years old before we ever had a car. I can remember some preacher used to come out to our house. I was a little old kid, but I can remember his wife was pregnant. Of course, I didn't know. Kids didn't know back then like they do now. But I spent the night at their house, and I know she told Mama, she said, "I was really surprised that you let Lucy come, knowing I was about ready to have that baby." That's about the first preacher I remember. His name was Brooks. And then Preacher Dail. Preacher Dail was here twice. When I was a little girl, Preacher Dail and his wife lived in a parsonage right next to the church house. They were such good people. It was just our church then, just the one church. We had morning services, night services and prayer meeting.

We used to just have a pastor, a regular pastor, because we had quite a few that went to the Methodist church – more than there are now. People who lived up at the state always came. The Kellys and Nelsons and Stockards and Stranges. The Comers – Clyde, Odeva, Paul, Peg and Beulah – went to the Methodist. Minnie Hatfield and her children. Irene Bradley. Dean ("D") and Georgie Ward. Just a lot of people. We had a good crowd. And young people too. But, you see, after the young people grew up, they moved off and nobody has any young children to come to our church anymore.

When Preacher Reagan Allison was our pastor – we had him full-time – we had a young people's group, the Epworth League. We had a good crowd that went to that. We had regular meetings and wiener roasts and little picnics and get-togethers. And then our church had a Ladies Aide Society. A lot of women would meet and quilt and have their meetings. Some women whose husbands maybe were miners or something like that had plenty of time to have their meetings, but Mama never had the time to take to do that. Ladies Aide eventually was the WSCS (Women's Society of Christian Service). Then I was old enough, with a family, and I started going to that. Georgie Ward was our president. She was real good.

We came to Sunday School and church every Sunday. I don't remember Dad and Leonard and Richard going as much as me and Mama and Lawrence did. Lawrence was the janitor out there at the church for awhile years ago. They had a coal stove, and he'd build fires, clean the church house up. We always had a church service on Thanksgiving Day too.

I remember Aunt Martha Taylor more than anybody being my Sunday School teacher. I don't really remember anybody much but her, so evidently as we grew up, she kept the same ones. We had a good size class. Later, Aileen Slaughter, Ed Bonifacius, Hattie Simpson, Elizabeth Strange and Alice Whitus taught our adult Sunday School class.

We had a choir and a piano and an organ. Leona Tucker led the singing a lot. Mrs. Dail, Preacher Dail's wife, played the piano when I was a kid. Then Aileen Slaughter played, and Flossie Bedford. Elizabeth Strange played when my children were growing up. And Mavis Carr. Imogene Evans. We sang, more or less, the same songs we sing now: "Amazing Grace" and "Just As I Am" and "Beautiful Garden of Prayer" and "In the Garden." My favorite song is "Whispering Hope." I love

"Whispering Hope" and "Beyond the Sunset." I think those two songs are really pretty. Lots of times Polly Woodward would play the organ and Imogene Evans would play the piano, and they would play that, and it would be so pretty. The church had an organ that you'd pump and play. You know those old-timey organs that you pumped? Of course now there's another organ out there. It belongs to Polly.

I really don't remember who was the superintendent of Sunday School when I was growing up. Seems like it was Jimmy Kelly. He lived up at the state. He was an electrician up there. And his wife played the piano some and taught a Sunday School class. After I was grown, Ed Bonifacius and Ralph Strange were superintendents. My son Pat was superintendent out there a long time too.

I asked Mom to tell me about when she joined the church.

Back then we would have revivals – maybe twice a year they would have a week or two-week revival – and it was in one of those meetings. They'd call people up, if you wanted to be saved, and you'd go sit down on the seat and somebody would come and talk to you. I remember Leona Tucker talking to me. And I did. I wanted to be. So I was. I must have been 10 or 11 or 12 years old. I was just a kid, but I can remember that. I was sprinkled at the church service the following Sunday. They would either sprinkle or baptize – the Methodists would do either one – but more or less we were sprinkled. I remember when I was sprinkled by Preacher Dail. He had a handful of water and he put it on top of my head. I can remember it running down my face and down my neck.

One of the things I remember about attending Petros Methodist Church was that people always seemed to wear their best clothes to church.

I don't notice that much change now, except hats were the fashion then – we wore hats a lot to church – and women never wore pants to church. In fact, when I was going to high school, we weren't allowed to wear pants to high school. I know one girl came to school one day with a pair of pants on, and they sent her home. She had to go home and put a dress on. I know when I was in elementary school, we wore that old long underwear. Oh, I hated that stuff. And you'd have long stockings. You'd put that underwear down in your stockings, and of course it would show, because girls wore dresses. But everybody did, so you weren't different from anybody else. But, girls never wore pants. I don't remember when that started. Of course they can wear whatever they want to now.

I can remember on Easter how my mom always got us a new dress and new petticoat and new shoes and new socks. New hat. New gloves. New purse. And she always had a corsage and a hat.

Some still wear corsages. I know Polly always has a big one on for every occasion, usually Bill gets her. But you seldom ever see hats anymore. Hats would be nice – they would hide your hair if it didn't look good. I know always on Easter, the church had an egg hunt on Sunday evening. Kids – and grownups too – would go out and hunt eggs.

One of my favorite memories is the "dinners" we used to have at church.

They were good, weren't they? A lot of times just after church service on Sunday, we'd have a big dinner, just to have them. On Christmas Eve we always have a Christmas Eve program. We would always have sandwiches and cakes and stuff like that down in the basement before the services. We've had the kitchen a long time now, but the kitchen used to be a classroom. Where the bathroom is now, that was a classroom. The men's bathroom and the women's bathroom takes up one that was a classroom. In fact, I think that was the classroom I was in when I was smaller. Then where the kitchen is now was the young people. Mrs. Douglass had a class there. Then there were three other classrooms. The older people stayed upstairs, and then all the younger people went downstairs.

The Methodist and Baptist churches have always been good neighbors.

In fact, a long time ago, the Methodist preacher would go down to the Baptist and hold a revival, and the Baptist preacher would come up there and preach sometimes. Doris West comes and plays our piano today – and her husband is the Baptist pastor. She's a good person.

In our family, Mom was a steward in the Methodist church and Daddy was a deacon/Sunday School superintendent/choir leader at the Baptist church.

We would go together some. He'd come with me a lot, and I would go with him. A lot of times I didn't have a preacher on Sunday night. Ours would just come – there for awhile it would be the first Sunday night and the second Sunday morning, third Sunday night and fourth Sunday morning. That's the way our pastors would be for awhile. And I would always go to the Baptist when we didn't have church. All of the kids, though, joined the Methodist church. Bill would go to the Baptist some, but I don't remember you other three going there at all.

I have been a church steward as long as I've been going, I guess. I was the Sunday School secretary before Pat was born. When Pat was born, Polly took it. Somebody asked her how long she had been secretary one day, and she said, "Lucy, how old is Pat?" That's how long she had been secretary. I took care of the Sunday School money, and I would order the literature. Then they had another one that paid the preacher, you know, had the church. Sunday School and church were kept separate, and I just had the Sunday School. I know Aunt Martha Taylor took care of the church. They said if she didn't have enough to pay the preacher out of the collection, she'd just take it out of her own pocket and pay him.

Lots of Sundays, you could find either a Methodist or Baptist preacher sitting at our table having lunch with our family.

Preachers used to go to your house and eat. They had to eat somewhere. Your daddy was on the Pulpit Committee at the Baptist church, and when they didn't have a pastor and they'd go out and get somebody to come and preach, he would bring them home with him. He'd bring them to the house. I remember it was dinner and supper both because they'd stay till that night. But it didn't bother us. We just let it go. People don't bother me; it's just the idea: "Do I have enough to eat?"

I can remember when I was in the seventh grade our school teacher made us memorize Bible verses. We had to memorize whole chapters. I can remember, seems like it's the 121st Psalm starts out, "I will lift up mine eyes unto the hills, from whence cometh my help. My help cometh from the Lord God who made heaven and earth." And then I know II Timothy 2:15, "Study to show thyself approved unto God, a workman that needeth not to be ashamed, rightly dividing the word of truth." Some of those verses just stick with me. We still have our benediction, that Psalm: "Let the words of my mouth and the meditation of my heart..." We still say that as our benediction at Sunday School now. Some verses stick with you.

Even if there's just a handful of us, it's still going to church. You get a blessing out of it.

SWEET MEMORIES

The Long family went to the Methodist church. Don Long was four years old when Woodrow and I got married. Don claimed me as his girlfriend, I reckon, and it made him mad because I got married. Then when I had Pat, he would hardly speak to me. We've kidded about that. Kids always pick some older person to have a crush on. Don thought I was his sweetheart, and he got mad at me when

I got married. We still laugh about that. Don is a Baptist preacher and has a church in Knoxville now.

When we were growing up, Richard would plow and work in the garden and just do things most anybody else did. But Mama and Dad were more protective of him because he had this affliction. He liked to go up "in town" we called it and sit around and talk to people. Some of them would tell him big tales, and he would think everything was whatever anybody told him. He just thought everybody told the truth all the time, I suppose.

But Richard had a fairly good life I would think. Everybody liked him. Everybody liked Richard. He helped himself a lot, but he missed Mama when she died. I would fix breakfast for him every morning, and then he would come down usually at suppertime and eat with us. But with four children, I just didn't have the room for him to live with us. But I did see that he didn't go hungry. And I would wash his clothes and iron them. He died in 1966, nine years after Mama died.

I never have liked storms. Mama and Dad always got up. I would stay in bed and cover my head up. I didn't get up, but anytime of the night if it came a storm they always got up and dressed. They stayed inside. They didn't act like they were afraid. They really didn't act scared. It was just their way of being. I don't know why. It's just what they did. And they would sit up till the storm was over. But I can remember staying in bed and covering my head up. Stopping my ears up too if I could so I couldn't hear it. I've never liked storms. I know of people yet that say they get up and put their clothes on when it's storming.

Sometimes the language of a person's childhood includes words and phrases that are not commonplace now. When I asked Mom to tell me about some of them, she mentioned these:

You don't ever hear anybody say "shuck beans." That was green beans that you would dry. We would put them on a string and hang them up on the wall behind the stove, or lay them out in the sun. They'd get real crispy dry. People would eat them in the wintertime. You would soak them overnight in water and they would swell. You would cook them just like you would ordinary beans with your seasoning and salt on them. They were good. They were real brown. Brown beans.

"Roasineers." *[That's corn-on-the-cob.]* And then some people call cornbread that you fix on top of the stove "hoe-cakes." Of course, there was always "sweet taters" instead of sweet potatoes. And back then you'd hardly ever say "Irish potatoes" – it was just "Arsh taters."

HOME REMEDIES AND OLD WIVES' TALES

Doctors would come to the house to treat you. I don't remember them giving shots. I guess they just gave us medicine. In fact, I don't remember any of us really being sick that much. We had measles. Probably whooping cough. But other than that, colds would be all we'd have. Seems like we had something that we put on our chest for a cold. They called it a "poultice," and it smelled to high heaven. But I don't know what was in it. I really don't. I remember us rubbing Vicks Salve on our chest and under our nose when our nose would get sore from blowing it so much. I still depend on Vicks Salve.

I reminded my mom that she swallowed it – and she made us kids swallow it too – for sore throats. Although the jar states specifically that you are not to ingest it, she informed me that she still does and that she has never suffered any harmful effects from it.

I'm still living. And it helps. When my throat would get sore – still yet – when my throat gets sore, if I just swallow a little Vicks Salve, it helps it.

People used to get turpentine. Turpentine is smelly stuff that was supposed to be good when you've got a sore or something like that, or if your bones ache. And liniment, the same thing. Liniment was strong-smelling. What you rub on now – like Flex-All and Icy Hot and that stuff – it has an odor to it too. That's just about what liniment smelled like back then. And alcohol. That was just more or less like a liniment or turpentine to rub your muscles when they were sore. When anybody would cough, they'd get rock candy (white-looking hard candy) and moonshine and – I can't remember what else was in it. There was something else called "Pain Destroyer." If you had a stomachache, you'd take a spoonful of that. And castor oil. I'm sure you've heard of castor oil. It makes you sick to even think about it. It was old slick, oily stuff. When I'd have to take a dose of castor oil, Mama would give me some coffee to drink. None of us drank coffee but my dad. It's a wonder I even like coffee.

Salesmen would go door to door – "peddlers" they were called back then – and sell stuff for the Watkins Company and the Raleigh Company and the Saymen's Company. I remember we bought Saymen's Salve. When you'd cut yourself or run into something or hit something, you'd get a sore, and Saymen's Salve was good for sores. Watkins was more or less liniment. I can remember Watkins Liniment. If their bones ached or something like that, they would rub themselves, where we get Flex-All and stuff like that now. It was a liniment. And people used to, if something got the matter with their horse's or mule's legs, if they acted like they were stiff, they'd rub them good with that Watkins Liniment. I don't remember what the Raleigh Company sold. I just remember that name.

And old wives' tales . . .

The only old wives' tale I can think of is if you were pregnant you should not look at anything or be around anything that took a chance on marking your baby. Once someone was having a seizure when I was at my in-laws' house. Mamaw said, "Don't look at her. Don't look at her." And I didn't. Really, that's about the only old wives' tale that I believed in, because I never did take a chance. In fact, when my father-in-law died, I was pregnant and I didn't look at him at all.

Those little wooly worms – if the worm was dark all over it would mean a cold hard winter, but if there was light at each end of it, it would just be real cold in the middle of the winter. And you will say, "If the sun sets red at night, it will be a pretty day." That's probably true because usually if there's a red sunset, you do have a pretty day the next day. And then a sunrise if it's red, the next day will be raining or a bad day. Fogs in August would mean that many snows in the winter. Seems like if a hornet's nest was built low on the ground, it would be a sign of cold weather.

WIDOWHOOD

In 1973, Woodrow hadn't felt good. He would come home from work and always want to lay down and rest a while. He was working, but he was just tired all the time. I know on Saturdays he would usually lay around and rest lots of the time. We were supposed to go to Missouri in May – we had our plane tickets and everything – when Leonard, my brother, got killed in a car wreck. We didn't go to Missouri. Woodrow went to Dr. Van Hook. He was yellow. We didn't know what it was; we thought maybe he had hepatitis or something. Dr. Van Hook put him in the hospital, and Dr. Stanley did exploratory surgery. We never thought about it being cancer. Not one time. But it was pancreatic cancer. Dr. Bigelow said he would not live long.

I asked Tommy Hensley, his pastor, if he would tell him. Tommy said, "I'll try." Then he told me, he said, "Lucy, I can't. I can't tell him he's got cancer and he's not going to live." Well, anyway, I had taken him over there to the doctor's office one day and Dr. Bigelow told him. I never will forget that day. I was sitting there waiting in the office, and he came out, and we got in the car and he started crying. He said, "Did you know?" And I said, "Yes, but I couldn't tell you. I couldn't tell you." But after he found out that he had it, it just seems like he started trying to do things then. Like he thought he was just sick and he was going to get well and he was just laying around taking care of himself. Then after he found out he had cancer, it seems like he just started trying to live then more so. I can recall many days you don't forget.

Woodrow Patrick, Lucy's husband.

We didn't make any plans – we just knew he wasn't going to get well – but we didn't talk about it. Our 30th wedding anniversary was on the 4th of July, 1974. We had a little party. I remember we were all sitting out on the porch and he stayed as long as he felt like it, then he went and lay down. He just kept gradually – well, you were there; you remember how he was. He died August 16, 1974. He was 60 years old.

Flouracil was the name of his medicine. Seems like it made him feel better. That's why Dr. Bigelow said he wanted to do the autopsy, to see if it had helped him. And it hadn't. It hadn't slowed the cancer a bit. But I remember Dr. Bigelow said, "Well, it did seem to make him feel better." And it did. He didn't get sick or lose his hair from the chemotherapy.

TODAY

To what does she attribute her good health?

Good genes, I guess, and clean living. I lived on a farm and was outside. We had good, clean air back then. I never did abuse my body. I have been lucky. I have, and I know it. I haven't had any major illnesses. I had a kidney stone in 1974. I had a benign lump in my breast in 1996 or 1997. I've been taking Lipitor for high cholesterol four or five years now. I had a high count as early as 1988, but

I had it down to 220. I just kind of quit eating so much greasy stuff and ice cream and candy and things that weren't good for me. But I still couldn't get it below 200, no matter what I did. So that's why I started taking the Lipitor.

I had cataracts taken off my eyes in 1997. They put lens implants in my eyes. I've been wearing glasses about 30 years. Actually, I guess I could make it without glasses, but I can't read without them. I started taking blood pressure medicine about three years ago. My blood pressure stays ok.

I never did drink, but I smoked a cigarette or two. No habit. Maybe once a week or something like that. I don't know how much I smoked. I didn't smoke much. I just did it for the heck of it. My mother didn't know it – I'll guarantee you that. In fact, I was grown – probably had you kids – the first cigarette I ever smoked. It was some of your daddy's cigarettes that I smoked. But I never did drink. I didn't like the stuff. None of it.

We were just healthy people. Just lucky people, I guess. We were outdoors a lot, but we had sense enough to put a coat and cap on when we went outside. You didn't go out inviting yourself to take a cold. It was colder then than it is now. I mean we really had wintertime when I was a kid growing up. More so than now. It would snow. It would be real cold. Usually by the middle of November it was real cold. Then probably December, January and February would be kind of cold. But then it started getting warm. I know Mama would always have a garden made in March. We'd have green lettuce and onions and mustard and all that good stuff early.

My favorite past-time now is reading. My favorite author is Emilie Loring. And I love to work crossword puzzles. That's the first thing I do of the morning. I go out and get my paper and work the crossword puzzle. I work the crossword puzzle every day. And, of course, I do read the Bible every day and my Bible readings. I watch TV, and I like to play cards. My favorite sports are baseball and softball. The Atlanta Braves used to be my favorite baseball team, but they've traded so many of their good players off, I don't know whether I even like them now or not. I will probably like the Mets now. Tommy Glavin's playing for the Mets. I would say he is my favorite player. When I was younger, shooting marbles and playing softball were my favorite sports to play.

My mom has always been the biggest sports fan – any sport – I've ever known. As a very, very little girl I remember seeing her sitting at the kitchen table with a radio, listening to boxing matches.

I like getting out and walking. I go to church. Go to our Senior Citizens meetings and Home Demonstration Club meetings. Love to go to good singings. Dollywood. I love to watch the Kingdom Heirs and the Gaithers. I love to listen to those programs. In fact, I have some of their videos and I really enjoy them. Movies – I believe I like *Steel Magnolias* better than any movie I've ever seen. I don't like bloody movies or scary movies. I like Sally Fields. And, of course, George Clooney. I like George Clooney. What else? Just being with people.

I depend on Mozell Duncan, my sister-in-law, more than anybody outside of my children. They come first and their families. My good friends – I have Alice Whitus and Peg Comer, of course. And I told somebody if I ever had a friend, Susie Waldrop was it. And Imogene Evans is really a good friend. I don't see her much now because she's not living in Petros, but she is a good friend to everybody. Jenny Lee Daugherty. I like people.

The man I most admire is Billy Graham. I think he's a good person. I watch all of his programs on TV, and I read his article in the paper each day. I have quite a few of his books.

I asked Mom what she thinks the world will be like 25 years from now.

I don't expect to be here, so I haven't really thought. I know when your dad was still living, he said, "I just worry about our children growing up, because the world is getting worse all the time." Well, it might be in some ways. But there will always be problems. Always be problems and troubles. That's just the way it is, I suppose. I think the world will be here in 25 years. But I told somebody one day, the end of the world is for you when you die. Of course if you believe the Bible, there will be an end of the world. But if you just think about it, when you die that's the end of the world for you.

What does she think heaven is like?

Well, we don't know – it's just what we read and what people project it is. But I think it will be a place where everybody will be happy. I've always said I regretted that I didn't learn how to play a piano. And I think, "Well, I'll play a piano when I get to heaven." If I'm lucky enough. And I'm trying to get there.

What does she think it takes to get to heaven?

Well, you've got to be born again. You've got to change. Your life has to change. And you don't get to heaven on your good deeds. I've read that so many times. Anybody should just live the best life they can and be good to people. Believe in God. If you believe strong enough, things happen for the best. I know a lot of my prayers have been answered. Have to be.

When I asked my mom where she would go if she could go anywhere in the world and do anything she wanted to do, her answer really tickled me.

I guess I would go to *The Price is Right* and *Wheel of Fortune*. I wouldn't mind being a contestant on *The Price is Right*, but *Wheel of Fortune* – my mind doesn't work that fast now. I like Bob Barker. In fact, I saw Bob Barker one time. We were at the fair in Knoxville, and we were sitting up in that open-air program, and he was on there. He passed by and patted you on the top of your head.

Being patted on the top of my head by Bob Barker is the closest brush I've had with a celebrity. Mom's yard, however, has been in a movie. In OCTOBER SKY, *the film version of Homer Hickam's book* ROCKET BOYS, *Mom's yard was the site where the boys' first rocket was launched. Her house was camouflaged, but her yard was used. That's as good as a pat on the top of the head.*

Petros came alive again for the filming of that movie in 1998. The town was transformed into a 1950s West Virginia mining town – not a hard stretch to make. Quite a few townspeople were extras. I was in Memphis when I saw the movie for the first time, and it was so exciting to watch for people and places I know. "There's Sue Ann Liles! There's Sadie Harris! There's Bill Christopher!" The movie lead's home was a house that sits on the main street of Petros.

For me, that movie is real close to what it was like growing up in Petros. I grew up seeing men in town covered with coal dust after getting off work in the mines.

My best friend growing up, Margaret Strange, lived with her mom and dad and sister Nancy at "the state." I spent lots of time at her house, near the prison. As children, we gave no thought to the prisoners working in the yard. It was just a normal part of our lives. Instead of playing "Cops and Robbers," some of us children in Petros played "Prisoner's Out."

It was the real-life Snow Blossoms – my mother (Lucy Patrick), Alice Whitus, Imogene Evans and Polly Woodward – who added beauty to Petros and made it a good place to grow up. They are the strong women who kept their families grounded and saw that all the children around them were cared for. They faced hardships in their personal lives and met those hardships head-on, surviving to become role models for generations following them. May the fragrance of these real-life Snow Blossoms always linger.

PHOTOGRAPH GALLERY

❄

Mothers of Snow Blossoms
Who Were Members of Petros Methodist Church Too

Emma Margaret Bardill Rogers Lehman, Polly's mother.

Mary America Cooley Whitus, Imogene's mother.

Annie Amaline Engert Joyner Duncan, Lucy's mother.

Annie Duncan, Lucy's mother, with granddaughter Nellie Claiborne and great-granddaughter Dorothy Jo Davis.

Emma and Bill Rogers, Polly's parents.

Emma and John Lehman, Polly's mother and stepfather.

Mary Whitus, Imogene's mother.

Gray Whitus, Imogene's father.

William and Lillian Bullock, Alice's parents.

The Snow Blossoms in 1994: Polly, Lucy, Imogene and Alice.

The Snow Blossoms 10 years later, in April 2004: Alice, Polly, Imogene and Lucy.

The Snow Blossoms in August 2004: Imogene, Polly, Alice and Lucy.

Petros United Methodist Church today. The first service in this church was held on Easter Sunday 1933. Prisoners at nearby Brushy Mountain Prison helped build the church.

Inside the Petros United Methodist Church today.

The still-beautiful chairs that the ladies society in the church paid to have reupholstered many years ago.

The old organ, no longer used, that Mrs. Hattie Simpson gave to the church.

An up-close shot of the little church "bank" where members place their birthday offering.

The Church Register of the Petros Methodist Episcopal Church, South, with records dating back to 1902.

A group from the Methodist church at the tower on the mountain above the prison in the 1930s. Front row: Emily Evans and Marie Scarbrough. Standing: Rev. Wilkinson (an evangelist holding a revival at the church), Leo Scarbrough, Dearie Scarbrough, Helen Scarbrough and Lucy Duncan. Young boy in back: Billy Scarbrough.

Pallbearers carrying the casket of 14-year-old William Riley ("Buster") Claiborne in August 1937 were members of the men's softball team. Buster had been their bat boy. Clockwise from left: Woodrow Patrick, Hurley Delaney, Lawrence Schubert, Eugene Woodward, Marvin Davis, Ed Taylor, Garland Edmond, unidentified, Elijah Patrick, Pat Hudson, Jud Bradley and John Schubert.

Petros Elementary School. Children in Petros attended this school, built in 1928, on Schoolhouse Hill until Petros-Joyner Elementary School was built in 1977.

N.D. Booher at age 90 in 1972. Mr. Booher was the depot agent in Petros and a member of the Methodist church.

Polly with the Rev. W.H. Dail, a much-loved pastor of the Methodist church.

> Tulip, Ark.
> Dec. 10, 1945.
>
> Pastor of M.E. Church,
> Petros, Tenn.
>
> The bearer hereof Mrs T.R. Whitus has been a acceptable member of the Methodist Episcopal Church, South in, Tulip Church Little Rock Conference.
>
> Otis Sutton P.C.
>
> Dear Alice: Am sending you your letter you can tear off from this note, we are very sorry to lose you from our church, but it is the right thing to do. Hope your husband is a good christian. We wish you both all the happiness there is to be had in this life. We are your friends Mr & Mrs Hugh Smith

Mrs. T.R. Whitus
Petros
Tennessee

Petros, Tenn.
Nov. 20 1930

The general state ogf the Church

1 think the Church is in pretty good condection,
We have started off very good for the year.
And 1 ame sure we will have a great year
    The Lord has given us several new members
for which we are thankful,and of course that helps a Church
in a spiritual way. No one wants to join any thing that is
dead,So we are much alive, and God is blessing in a wonderful
way, We are expecting to take on some more new members soon.
1 think the Church is getting to a place now where she can do
somthing for the glory of God, God has given us members that 1
think will be a great hepp to the Church,For before a Church can
go there must be some body behind it, 1 think we are just now
entering the promise land,But there is more land to possesse.
And 1 ame sure that God is speaking to us that we go forward.

E.R.Allison
E.R.Allison,Pastor

Pictures of Petros, ca. 1908, from the Farnham Collection

View from H&N Train Depot toward state mines. Note the rock ledges on right that are still a landmark in Petros. None of the buildings in this picture exist today. Church members held services in Bedford's Store, the two-story building farthest back, while the current Methodist church was being built.

Street view in Petros. ① Bank, ② Opera House (the small building next to it is Bob Martin's Barbershop; ③ Big Brushy Commissary.

Street and mountain view from Big Brushy Commissary. ① Barbershop; ② Riley and Martha Taylor's Store; ③ White Hall; ④ Portwood's House; ⑤ Baptist Church; ⑥ Opera House; ⑦ Drugstore.

Powerhouse and miners' houses of Big Brushy Coal and Coke Company.

Big Brushy Coal and Coke Company's Tipple and Powerhouse. This is in the present-day vicinity of Ten Row.

Petros Today

Petros lies at the end of a valley protected on three sides by mountains. The house on the right was used for the filming of *October Sky*.

Some of the rock ledges that likely inspired the naming of the town. These rocks are on the hill below Lucy Patrick's house.

More rock formations below the prison warden's home.

Brushy Mountain Correctional Complex (formerly known as "Brushy Mountain Prison").

Two of the relatively few remaining houses at "the state."

THE TOWN

THE CHURCH

AND THE PENITENTIARY

❋

THE TOWN

Petros is pronounced *pee-tross*. It's one of those names that newscasters – and others we think should know better – often mispronounce. The closest word I've seen that resembles the name of the town is *petrous*. The definition of *petrous* is: *adj. Resembling stone; hard*. It is said that the name of Petros is derived from the Greek word *petra* meaning "rock." A drive through Petros reinforces the belief that that is indeed why Petros is called Petros. There are several prominent rock formations in the town.

Petros is in the eastern portion of Morgan County, Tennessee. It is at the end of a valley protected by mountains: Brushy, American Knob, Frozen Head and Windrock. Cherokee Indians first inhabited the land that is now Morgan County. After the land was freed from Indian claims (1816 through 1818), white people began to settle the area. Many of the early settlers were Revolutionary War soldiers who received their land from the government as a reward for military service. In 1817, Morgan County was established and named in honor of Gen. Daniel Morgan, a Revolutionary War officer and U.S. Congressman from Virginia. It was created from parts of Roane and Anderson counties. Later, parts of Morgan were taken to form Fentress, Scott and Cumberland counties.

The population of Morgan County is 19,847 according to the latest census records. The population of Petros is estimated to be less than 1,000.

The town of Petros was first called "Richburg," and the post office there was called "Joynersville." According to the authors of *A History of Morgan County*, the name of the post office was changed from "Joynersville" to "Petros" by an order of the Post Master dated December 4, 1895. However, deeds in the Morgan County Deed

Book refer to the "Village of Richburg" until 1906. The town was first called "Petros" in the Morgan County Deed Book on April 23, 1906.

The little village was a farming community until the discovery of coal seams in the area in the late 1800s and the building of Brushy Mountain Prison in 1895/1896 transformed it into a bustling town with schools, churches, lodges, an opera house, bank, drugstore, restaurant, bakery, pool hall, barber and beauty shop, and a number of stores. For a few years, two trains a day hauled coal being mined in the area.

Townspeople primarily supported their families by farming, mining coal or working at the prison. During World War II, buses transported workers to Oak Ridge, 20 miles away, to work at the wartime plants that grew up there.

Shortly after World War II, the coal market declined. Mines around Petros were eventually depleted. Although the last prison-operated coal mine was closed in 1966, the prison itself continued to operate, and it is still in operation today. However, the state plans to close Brushy once an expansion of the Morgan County Regional Correctional Facility in Wartburg is complete. Officials project the expansion will be completed in 2007. A number of residents continue to work in Oak Ridge at the government plants operated by the Department of Energy.

The Petros that is the background for much of the reminiscence by the ladies in this book is quite different from the Petros of today. The days the town was incorporated, with its own mayor and city council, are long past. While Petros still has several churches and a couple of stores, it is not the bustling town it once was. When you do a search about Petros on the Internet, you find that Petros has two claims to fame: (1) James Earl Ray, convicted killer of Martin Luther King, Jr., escaped from Brushy Mountain Prison in 1977 (and was captured after a three-day chase); and (2) the movie *October Sky* was partially filmed in Petros in 1998.

THE CHURCH

The first Methodist church in Petros was built in 1903 under the direction of Pastor James M. Jimison. This excerpt written by Dr. E.E. Wiley, Sr., Presiding Elder, from the *1909 Official Record of the Holston Annual Conference, Methodist Episcopal Church, South,* captures eloquently and beautifully the essence of this first pastor and first church:

James M. Jimison

At noon on the 16th of February, at Erlanger Hospital in Chattanooga, James Manley Jimison died in peace. He was closing out the thirty-second year of his age, having been born on the 10th day of April, 1877. His birthplace was near Asheville, N.C., where both parents and his brothers and sisters now reside. His brother, T.P. Jimison, was at his bedside during his last hours.

He was a young man of vigorous mind, incessant energy, unusual devotion to his conceptions of right, and possessed of pleasing social qualities. He was always busy at something good, and it was the everlasting force that he put into the work assigned him that brought him to his grave in such an early year. But he was as gentle as he was strenuous. No man among us was easier of approach or more apparent in his sincerity. While older ones hesitated not to confide in him, the children literally gave him their hearts. There was something in the motions of his body, the flash of his eye, his energetic way of putting things that charmed a child. A little fellow, none too fond of sitting through service-hour, heard the first sermon he ever preached. The text was, "The slothful man saith, there is a lion in the way." The child expressed himself as wanting to hear him preach again, and upon being asked why, replied, "He tells about lions."

Jimison's life was one continuous campaign marked by many struggles. The circumstances of his home were such as to render impracticable the granting to him of any financial aid for an education beyond the public schools. His conversion in childhood seems to have been accompanied by a consciousness of his call to the ministry. He felt that this was also a call to preparation through mastery of a course of study in the class rooms of a Christian College. Here was perhaps the initial struggle of his career. I saw him for the first time in the summer of 1898, as I now remember, on the farm of Emory and Henry College, working to meet the expense of a school year which was to begin the following September. My admiration for him began at that moment and has continued, without interruption, up to this hour. Along with it have grown a friendship and a personal love that compelled for me an overwhelming sense of loss in his – humanly speaking – untimely departure.

His college days were days of improvement. He applied himself to his studies, took a keen interest in the debates of his literary society, cultivated his professors, and sought the counsel and the confidence of the President, Dr. Waterhouse, whom of all men next to his own family, he held in highest esteem. But for failing health, he would have remained in school until graduation. As it was, he pursued his course of study until well into his junior year. His gratitude to the college never for a moment abated, and the estimate he put upon the favors he received from Emory and Henry could not easily be described. I believe he would cheerfully have given the last penny of personal property he possessed for her assistance, if seriously called upon to do so. And many a time did he mention his desire to sleep at the last under the sod of the old cemetery whose pines stand as lonely sentinels guarding the valley and adjacent hill, whereon are laid the foundations of this institution of learning. And there he sleeps.

He served four charges in Holston Conference. In the summer of 1901 he completed the unexpired year of W.P. Buhrman at Lenoir City, who was transferred to the West. His second charge was Petros. In 1905 he was appointed to Rockwood, and the following year to South Pittsburg, of which church he was pastor at the time of his death. His pastorate at Petros was noteworthy. He was called to this mining field when there was neither a member to preach to, nor a house in which to preach. And yet in the space of two and one-half years he built up a Sunday School with an enrollment of 168, a membership numbering 52, erected and paid for a most creditable church building and a parsonage-cottage for his own convenience and comfort. In addition to this he looked after the spiritual welfare of some 800 prisoners in the Brushy Mountain stockades, having been appointed Chaplain there by James B. Frazier, then Governor of Tennessee. Many loyal and generous friends interested themselves in our project there, but the beginning was a matter of experiment and uncertainty. It appeared as if he had laid siege to Port Arthur – but if such it was, he did not let up until it fell into his hands.

I asked him a few months ago what he would have done, had he failed to secure a foothold there at that time. He answered in the most matter of fact sort of way that he would have worked in the mines through the week and preached to the people on Sunday. Those who knew Jimison at all well doubt not that he would have done that thing.

In his methods of thinking he was concise and analytical. His mind worked quickly and comprehensively. If he prepared his sermons with speed, he showed in their delivery that he had gone over the ground thoroughly and drawn his conclusions with care. His opinions on moral questions amounted to convictions and he defended the position he took with vigor and pertinacity. In his pulpit utterances he gave no quarter to sin. He rebuked it with a fervor that rarely failed to stir his hearers and arouse the sinner from the drowsy spell into which he had been lulled. At the same time, he was tender with the frailties of men and made much of the love of God in his appeals to them.

The explanation of his multitude of accomplished plans lay in the complete consecration of the man to God. The one question with him was, "Ought this to be done?" And if he answered affirmatively, he gave himself wholly to his task. Besides bringing to bear upon it the strength of an unalterable purpose, he called into requisition a virile faith in the promises of the Word, constant prayer, and ever present disposition to give the glory of his achievement to God....

How very brief, and yet how very full, was this life! So brief indeed that we pause, and with pressed lips and bated breath, wonder why; and yet so rich and so full that we will not dare to doubt that it was a life at once finished and complete. Of him it is true, as was said of another, that he always and everywhere gave his strength to the weak, his substance to the poor, his sympathy to the suffering, his heart to God.

The Methodist Episcopal Church, South, built in Petros under Pastor Jimison, was torn down almost 30 years later, and a new building was erected. Church members attended services in Bedford's old store building that stood near the current-day Masonic Hall until the new church was completed. The church was built with prison labor and cost approximately $3,000. The first service in the new church was held on Easter Sunday 1933. It is this still-beautiful church that the few but faithful members attend today.

In 1939 the Northern and Southern Methodist Episcopal Churches and the Methodist Protestant Church merged to form the Methodist Church. Then in 1968 the Methodist Church and the Evangelical United Brethren Church united to form the United Methodist Church. Since that time, the church in Petros has been known as "Petros United Methodist Church."

Ministers at the church were at first assigned solely to the Petros church. Later, circuit riders in the fashion of John and Charles Wesley served Petros along with Jonesville and Dutch Valley. Today the circuit is Petros, Jonesville and Oliver Springs. Early pastors lived in a parsonage in Petros. Today, pastors live in a parsonage in Oliver Springs provided in part by the church.

The church has been served by many pastors through the years. Relying on *The Church Register of the Petros Methodist Episcopal Church, South,* and the memories of the Snow Blossoms, we came up with this list of pastors who have tended the flock at Petros since 1902, and the years of their appointment, if known:

J. M. (James) Jimison (1902-1904)	French Taylor
J. Y. Bowman (1905-1907)	M. Latham
D.V. York	Pastor Chambers
W. T. Evans (1908)	C.C. (Charlie) Bray (1945)
Fred B. Cox (1910)	Ernest Howard (1957)
W. E. Hightower (1912)	R. R. (Ronald) Ratcliffe (1962)
Pastor Shelley (1912)	Everett Johnson (1966)
E. R. Roach (1913)	Pastor Beaty
A. L. Perkins (1916)	L. T. Carden (1971)
S. A. McCandless (1917)	W.T. Carey (1973)
Pastor White	Ed Nelson (1980s, 1990s)
S. L. Dyke	Herbert Hoover
R. N. (Rufus) Brooks (1921)	Harvey Mason
William H. Dail (1926, 1950, 1961)	Ronald Burgess
E. R. (Reagan) Allison (1929)	Malcolm Walmsley
E. B. Randall (1937)	Bobby Barton (current pastor)
Austin White	

Church records reflect that the first members of the church in 1903 were: James M. Jimison, Nellie Joyner, Martha Choat, Mrs. R.L. Blevins, James H. Rogers, Charles R. Ridinger, Cora Whitus, Ed Whitus, Joseph P. Raynor, John Whaley, Frank Baker, Verdie Baker, Naoma Baker, Lola Hudson, Mattie Bender, William Z. Greene, Lola Ledford, Nora Duff, Lavinia Whitus, Betty Whitus, Mary Franklin, Thomas Byrd, Dora Byrd, Harry Brown and Mary Brown.

Infant baptisms in 1903 included: Laura, Mary, Katheryn, Bert and Josephine Joyner; Lillie Anne and John Frances Choat; Earl Williams; William Copeland; Lalina May Gertrude Brown; Annie, Cecil and William Bender; and Zola Byrd.

When you look around the church, you can feel the spirit of long-ago members. Inscriptions on plaques next to the nine upstairs windows in the church read:

> N.D. Booher and Family
> Rev. W. H. Dail and Family
> In Memory of Martha E. Taylor
> In Memory of Annie E. Duncan
> In Memory of Maudie J. Claiborne
> In Memory of Ramsey Perley Daugherty
> In Memory of E.H. Bonifacius
> Wilma Tucker and Ruth Tucker Wood
> In Memory of W.P. Rogers

Inscriptions on plaques next to the downstairs windows in the church read:

> In Memory of J.F. Simpson
> In Memory of Edward Watkins
> Presented by Methodist Youth Fellowship

An inscription under the lighted cross at the front of the church reads: "In Memory of Joseph and Ellen Daugherty, Given by Frazier Daugherty and Family." A picture of "Tennessee's Rural Minister of the Year 1961 - Rev. W.H. Dail" hangs under the clock in the sanctuary.

The Epworth League mentioned by several of the ladies in this book was a Methodist youth organization formed in 1889. Its motto was "All for Christ." The Epworth League was named for Epworth, England, birthplace of John Wesley. John Wesley (1703-1791) was an English theologian and evangelist, and founder of Methodism.

In 1939, the Epworth League's name was changed to the Methodist Youth Fellowship (MYF). After World War II, the MYF instituted short-term mission projects in Japan, Africa and India. Along with home missions, these programs are viewed by many historians as being the direct predecessors of the Peace Corps and VISTA programs in the 1960s. In 1968, the name was changed to the United Methodist Youth Fellowship (UMYF).

THE PENITENTIARY

The story of Petros United Methodist Church would not be complete without including information about the prison located in Petros. All of the ladies I've written about had relatives – fathers, husbands, brothers or children – who worked at the prison at one time or another. Many, if not most, of the early members of the Methodist church in Petros were employees of the prison. Prisoners built the church.

Today, in 2004, the prison is known as the Brushy Mountain Correctional Complex (BMCX). It has the distinction of being the state's oldest operating prison. The State of Tennessee is the chief employer in Morgan County.

In interviews, the women often referred to "the state." This phrase – "the state" – still today is synonymous with the prison. "State people" are employees of the prison. Local people know that if a family lives "at the state," that means they live on the grounds (owned by the State of Tennessee) outside the prison.

Ruth Winton (1904-1999) was born and raised in Petros. During her long career as an educator, she was a teacher, an elementary school principal and the superintendent of Morgan County Schools. She taught schools in Petros, Wartburg, Joyner and Oak Ridge. In Oak Ridge, she taught at Elm Grove, Cedar Hill and Pine Valley elementary schools and at Robertsville Junior High School.

As part of the requirements for a Master of Arts degree with a major in history at the University of Tennessee, Ruth Winton wrote her thesis on Brushy Mountain Penitentiary. Her thesis, submitted in 1937, contains a fascinating history of the prison in Petros. The following is information gleaned from "Miss Ruth's" thesis:

On January 1, 1831, the first penitentiary in Tennessee was opened near Nashville. From 1831 through 1865, prisoners were employed on public works inside and outside the prison. For example, prisoners helped build the State Capitol and they made supplies for the Confederate Army during the Civil War. Prison officials could not keep enough raw materials on hand, so many convicts were idle much of the time.

"The ravages of war rendered the prison buildings uninhabitable." The state was in debt, and complicating matters was the fact that the legislature had not made provisions for maintenance of the prison. It became necessary to devise a plan to make the prison self-sustaining and provide for the ever-growing number of prisoners. In late 1865, a legislative committee decided unanimously in favor of a convict leasing system. In 1866, the legislature enacted a law authorizing penitentiary officials to lease out the penitentiary.

In July 1866, a four-year contract was awarded to Hyatt, Briggs and Moore, the highest and best bidder, to occupy and take charge of all the shops and workhouses in the prison and to install whatever machinery was necessary to manufacture reapers, mowers, thrashers, hames, harnesses, saddles, plows, wagons and cedarware. In return, Hyatt, Briggs and Moore was "to hire all the able-bodied convicts in the prison except those that were necessary for the maintenance of the penitentiary." Hyatt, Briggs and Moore would pay 43 cents a day for each convict, and the state would pay for guarding, feeding, housing and clothing the convicts with funds derived from the labor of the convicts. This arrangement looked promising.

However, in June 1867, a fire destroyed buildings, raw materials and finished products. The result was a financial deficit at the close of the year instead of a profit. Hyatt, Briggs and Moore built a new workshop within the prison and carried on with their manufacturing. Mechanical industries in the state, which had to compete with convict-made goods and then prison-trained mechanics released from prison, complained. The state listened. Beginning in 1871, many convicts were put to work on railroads and in coal mines. It was difficult to guard prisoners working on the railroads, and many escaped, so convicts working on railroads were sent to the coal mines where escapes were rare.

Working convicts in the coal mines served two purposes. It was a method of (1) making the prisoners pay for their upkeep, and (2) developing the mineral resources of the state.

Despite some objections, for the most part state officials and the public were so satisfied with the convict lease system that had proven profitable to the state that the system was continued. In 1889, a new contract was made with the Tennessee Coal, Iron and Railroad Company. Prisoners were put to work in the coal mines near Oliver Springs, Coal Creek, Briceville, Tracy City and Inman.

The use of convicts in the mines, along with other grievances the miners had, led to a number of strikes, insurrections and revolts by the coal miners in 1891 and 1892. During these insurrections, miners released prisoners, destroyed stockades and buildings, or loaded the prisoners on trains and sent them to either Knoxville or Nashville. It took the state militia to maintain law and order. The riots caused great financial loss to the state and endangered the lives of many people.

In 1893, the General Assembly passed an act abolishing the convict lease system, with an expiration date of January 1, 1896. The "Penitentiary Act of 1893" provided for construction of a new penitentiary and for the purchase of farm and coal lands.

The main prison in Nashville could accommodate only 500 of the 1,400 state prisoners, so the stockades at Big Mountain (Oliver Springs), Tracy City and Inman that had been destroyed during the coal miners' insurrections were rebuilt and convicts remained there until the lease system was abolished and a new prison could be built. The prison camp at Big Mountain was discontinued in July 1894, and the inmates and guards were moved to a railroad camp near Harriman.

In 1894, the state paid $80,000 to the East Tennessee Land Company for 9,000 acres of coal lands in the Brushy Mountains in Morgan County at Joynersville (known today as Petros). Work began on a stockade to house prisoners who were to work in the mines and on development of the coal seams. The first Brushy Mountain Penitentiary was constructed as an L-shaped wooden building, entirely surrounded by high mountains that formed a narrow triangle, to accommodate about 600 prisoners. A gate entrance, with a guard shack built over it, and a "manway" though which prisoners passed to the mines were the only two openings.

On January 1, 1896, with the expiration of the convict lease system, half of the convicts who had been working in the coal mines at Coal Creek and Tracy City were transferred to Brushy Mountain Penitentiary in Petros. The other half were taken to the state penitentiary in Nashville as there was not yet enough working space in the mines at Petros to use them. "In all, there were 329 prisoners confined at Brushy Mountain Penitentiary at first. As working space in the mines developed, the number was increased. By December 1, 1896, there were 466." By 1904, the average convict population incarcerated at Brushy numbered 700.

"Since the building was made of lumber that had not yet become seasoned, it was extremely damp, and the weather during January and February of 1896 was such that there were many deaths from exposure and pneumonia." When the prison first opened, it was lighted with kerosene lamps suspended from the ceiling, supplemented by smaller ones around the sides of the rooms. In 1899 these oil lamps were replaced with electric lights, an electric haulage system was installed in the mines, a floor was built in the dining room, and other improvements "for the sake of the health, comfort and safety of the prisoners" were made.

During the ensuing years, many expansions and improvements were made to the prison, and new buildings were constructed to address the growing needs of the prison. In addition to the physical plant, the prison had a 60-acre garden (and hundreds of acres of other farm land that it rented/share-cropped), farm animals, a barn, feed mill, potato house, sawmill and cannery.

Other buildings were constructed for employees of the prison: a retail commissary, dormitories for guards, houses for employees' families and a school for the children of employees. The school, also used for church and lodge meetings, was discontinued in 1914.

From 1899 until the federal prison in Atlanta was built, the state had a contract to incarcerate federal prisoners as well at Brushy Mountain. In all, from 500 to 700 federal prisoners served time at Brushy. The federal government paid the state 25 cents a day for the maintenance of each prisoner.

More than two-thirds of the prisoners at Brushy were required to work in the coal mines. Their task was "usually the equivalent of loading from two to six tons of coal a day, depending on the thickness of the coal, or working twelve hours a day six days a week at some other task.... Men who wished to earn extra money might do so by working 'over task,' being paid from five to forty cents a ton for loading coal." When Brushy opened in 1896, only one mine was in operation. Five additional mines were eventually opened. Coal mined by the prison was to be used by the state for government buildings and state institutions only.

Beginning around 1911 and lasting into the 1920s, prisoners from Brushy also worked on state and county highways. In 1916, Campbell County employed 225 prisoners for a dollar a day to construct the Jellico Highway toward LaFollette. Another 125 worked as timber cutters. Prison camps were established at Morley and High Cliff for highway operations and at Fork Mountain for timber operations.

It was estimated that more than 60 percent of the inmates were illiterate, and more than 75 percent had no religious belief. Those who could neither read nor write were required to attend a night school program under the direction, at different times, of Rev. R.N. Brooks and Rev. E.R. Allison. [Author's note: These men were ministers at the Methodist church in Petros.]

By 1931, 976 prisoners were housed in the old frame penitentiary built in 1895, and the penitentiary was described as "a most dangerous fire hazard" with conditions approaching those "which prevailed in the Siberian prisons under the old Russian regime." In 1933-1934, the old prison was replaced by a new structure made of reinforced concrete in the shape of a Greek cross with battlements on top. Stone mined from a quarry near the prison was used to build the 18-foot-high wall surrounding the prison. Construction was performed by both convict labor and CWA labor. [Author's note: The CWA – Civil Works Administration – was part of Franklin D. Roosevelt's New Deal program between 1933 and 1935.] After the new prison was built, 640 prisoners moved into the new facility and the right wing of the old prison was torn down. However, as there were more than 900 prisoners at Brushy Mountain, the remaining 300 prisoners were at first kept in the old frame structure and then moved to the auditorium of the new concrete building until a new prison was built in Pikeville to relieve the crowded conditions at Brushy.

The days are long gone when prisoners mined coal or made leather purses and wallets at Brushy Mountain. Although the prison continues to have a maximum security designation, today it serves as the reception/classification and diagnostic center for East Tennessee and houses all custody levels. Some current staff members are fifth-generation employees.

The Morgan County Regional Correctional Facility (MCRCF) was established in 1980 and is located near what used to be known as Brushy Mountain Prison's "Honor Farm" on the road that leads to Frozen Head State Park near Wartburg. This time-building institution has a security designation of minimum restricted. Expansion of this regional prison site is projected to begin in 2005 and be completed in 2007. The expansion will create 1,428 additional beds and will generate 138 new jobs for the region. Once the expansion is complete, the state plans to close the prison in Petros.

Community service crews from both institutions perform thousands of hours of labor for local government and non-profit organizations each year.

It remains to be seen what will become of the historic prison in Petros once it closes and how the closing of the prison will change the character of the town itself. One thing is for sure: this unforgettable town is home to some unforgettable people.

THE END

BIBLIOGRAPHY

Author's interview with Imogene Evans, November 11, 2003, April 1, May 4, 2004, in Knoxville, Tennessee.

Author's interview with Lucy Patrick, January 21, February 11, February 18, 2003, March 11, 2004, in Petros Tennessee; February 1, February 2, April 27, June 14, 2003, in Knoxville, Tennessee.

Author's interview with Alice Whitus, January 21, February 1, February 18, May 31, June 9, 2003, March 11, May 5, 2004, in Petros, Tennessee.

Author's interview with Polly Woodward, February 2, February 11, June 1, June 9, 2003, in Petros, Tennessee.

"Brushy Mountain Correctional Complex," http://www.state.tn.us/correction/institutions/bmcx.

Church Registers of the Petros Methodist Episcopal Church, South (later called Petros United Methodist Church), 1902-1990.

"Epworth League," http://www.wisconsinumc.org/sunprairieumc/history/youth.

Freytag, Ethel, and Glena Kreis Ott, *A History of Morgan County Tennessee.* Specialty Printing Company, 1971.

Miner, William Dilworth, *Surrender on Cebu: A POW's Diary - WWII.* Paducah, Kentucky: Turner Publishing Company, 2001.

Morgan County News, 1999, 2000, 2004.

Oak Ridger, 1999.

Sakowski, Carolyn, *Touring the East Tennessee Backroads.* Winston-Salem, North Carolina: John F. Blair, Publisher, 1993.

Shipwash, Nellie Langley, *Petros: A Journey Back.* Clinton, Tennessee: Clinton Courier-News.

Wiley, E. E., "James M. Jimison,"*Official Record of the Holston Annual Conference, Methodist Episcopal Church, South, 86th Session, Johnson City, Tennessee, October 6-12, 1909*, pp. 75-77.

Winton, Ruth Nelle, "Brushy Mountain Penitentiary." Unpublished thesis, University of Tennessee, 1937.

ABOUT THE AUTHOR

JUNE GIBBS (born Alice June Patrick) was raised in Petros and grew up in the Petros United Methodist Church. She graduated from Tennessee Technological University in Cookeville with a Bachelor of Science degree in secondary education. She lives in Knoxville with her husband, Steve Gibbs. Their blended family includes children: Nikki Vanderyt, Erin Webb, Casey Shelton, Ginger Cronogue and Chris Gibbs; sons-in-law: Brad Webb, Kurt Vanderyt and Harry Cronogue; and grandchildren: Caden, Caroline and Conlin Webb, Olivia Vanderyt and Jacob Cronogue. She is newsletter editor for the Knoxville chapter of the Compassionate Friends.

Snow Blossoms

ORDER FORM

I would like to order _____ copies of *Snow Blossoms: The Ladies of Petros United Methodist Church*. The purchase price is $18.50 per copy. This pays for the book, sales tax, postage and handling.

Please send check or money order to:

June Gibbs
PO Box 6412
Oak Ridge, TN 37831-6412

Please send book(s) to the following address(es):

Name_____

Street or PO Box_____

City_____

State_____ Zip Code _____

Please list any special inscription you would like in the book:

_____

❄ ❄ ❄ ❄ ❄ ❄ ❄ ❄

Name_____

Street or PO Box_____

City_____

State_____ Zip Code _____

Please list any special inscription you would like in the book:

_____